The Sacred Heart of Jesus

By Fr. Marin de Boylesve, S.J.

The Sacred Heart of Jesus

By Fr. Marin de Boylesve

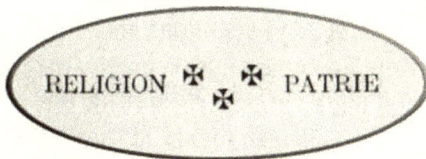

RELIGION ✠ ✠ PATRIE

Translated and annotated
by E.A. Bucchianeri

Batalha Publishers
Fatima, Portugal

This first English translation edition is based on the 1877 French edition published by Jules Vic, Paris. Rue Cassette. The translation, added biography of the author, annotations and appendix by E.A. Bucchianeri, © 2021-2022 by Batalha Publishers, Portugal. Appendix features traditional Roman Catholic prayers and quotations in the public domain.

ISBN: 978-989-33-2807-1

Table of Contents

II. The Heart of Jesus and the Word

III. The Heart of Jesus and the Holy Spirit

Appendix

Indulgenced Prayers to the Sacred Heart

About this Edition

This new English translation is based on the 1877 French edition published by Jules Vic, Paris. Rue Cassette. Apparently, this is the first ever English translation, British spelling has been used. This edition contains a biography of the author not in the French edition, also, annotations are new. Several devotional illustrations not in the original have been included, as well as the devotions and prayers in the Appendix.

E.A. Bucchianeri

About the Author

Fr. Marin de Boylesve was born on November 28, 1813 at the Château de la Coltrie in the commune of Saint-Lambert de la Potherie near Angers. He came from a distinguished aristocratic family whose name can be traced back many centuries as seen in Abbé Jean-Baptiste Ladvocat's *Dictionnaire historique portatif* (1755). Fr. Marin descended directly from Eslienne Boyliaue (or Boilyeve), the great statesman and the principal adviser of St. Louis IX, King of France. Other illustrious ancestors included intrepid knights, one in particular also named Marin joined the cause of King Henry IV. After the Battle of Arques, the king called him 'his beloved knight', granted him a heredity knighthood in 1597, then was made Seigneur de la Maurouziere in 1598 thereby granting him the right to add three gold fleur-de-lis to the top of his arms and bear the signs of the Order of St. Michel in his escutcheon. He was also appointed lieutenant-general of Anjou and councillor of state as a reward for his dedication. Another Marin Boylesve appears in the family line, the third to hold the name, and was in service to King Louis XIV as manager of his hôtel. Loyal to the French King and to their Catholic faith, many members of the family were forced to emigrate during the French Revolution, but some members stayed behind in their beloved France. Fr. de Boylesve would recall a favourite family story, of how his grandmother was imprisoned in Angers by the Revolutionaries and managed a daring escape on the road during a prisoner transfer to the local castle. While she pretended to pick up a dropped package, a solider kicked her into the ditch. She took the opportunity to flee to a nearby house. However, when they threatened to imprison those harbouring escaped prisoners, she bravely marched straight in to the Revolutionary Office and gave herself up to ensure the safety of those who sheltered her. The revolutionaries did not dare risk upsetting the populace as her father was the former mayor of Angers before the Revolution and loved by the people. They decided to let her return to her father's house.

Fr. de Boylesve was the last direct descendant of his distinguished line, having followed the call to enter the Company of Jesus, or Jesuits, which also is a remarkable story of a predestined vocation. The Jesuits were persecuted due to fears they were growing in power and wealth. Pressured by the royal courts of Europe, Pope Clement XIV suppressed the Society, forcing members of the order to renounce their vows and go into exile. They were expelled from France in 1764. Fr. de Boylesve's mother, Clémentine de Livonnière, made a solemn promise on the day of her wedding that if God permitted the Jesuits to return to France and she was granted a son, she would offer him to the order and entrust him to it. As mentioned, Fr. Marin was born in 1813, a year before 1814 when Pope Pius VII restored the Society. Tragedy struck when Marin's father died, Marin was only ten months old at the time, but keeping her promise his mother dutifully sent him for his education at the age of ten to the Jesuit Fathers of Montmorillon. The moment he arrived at the school and saw a Jesuit for the first time who happened to be the Superior of the college Fr. Michel Le Blanc, he heard an inner voice say to him: "Little one, that is what you will be."

Fr. de Boylesve entered the school as a student and was destined never to leave the Jesuits. In 1831 he turned eighteen, a year after the July Revolution of 1830, which saw the rightful king to the French throne Charles X overthrown. His heir, Henry V the 'Miracle Child', was forced into exile at the age of ten, his throne usurped by the man who had been approached to be his regent, Louis-Philippe, Duke of Orléans. The events of the times burned the hearts of the faithful as the historical church of the royal family, Saint-Germain-l'Auxerrois, was profaned. Paris was sacked, and wayside devotional crosses and shrines over large areas of France were destroyed as Catholic legitimist symbols of Charles X, even those which had no royal significance or connection to the king.

Fr. Marin had just completed his schooling when he formally announced his decision to enter the Society, the historic events of the previous year and their aftermath no doubt influencing his decision. Writing to his grandmother he declared: "The course of my studies completed I could not remain without doing anything. God will ask us for an exact account of all the moments He gives us. Full of this thought I ardently wished to serve my country and the Church especially. At a time when both are in such great peril, as a Frenchman and as a Christian, I felt the need to throw myself into the thick of the fray. To take place in the first rows under the banners of religion whose triumph alone can bring glory and happiness back to my homeland, to serve immediately under my first head Jesus Christ, to be one of His companions, seemed to me the most glorious at the same time as most useful for my neighbour. Immense advantages, treasures of happiness and glory, the hundredfold from this life of all that I would give to the Lord, all of these promised in the gospel by Jesus Christ, strongly attracted me to be generous. What more could I do than give myself? (...)"

His family strongly opposed, especially as he was the last direct heir to the Boylesve house, but his mother let him go despite the great sacrifice, no doubt she understood God was accepting her promise to give him to the Jesuits, and not just for his education but now was asking for his whole life, a bitter dreg for her down to the last drop of the cup.

He entered the Novitiate in 1831 at Estavayer in the canton of Fribourg in

Switzerland with two other students. As they arrived at their new school, they rang the doorbell at the moment the house clock struck three. The Father who received them remarked: "You are entering at the hour of the Sacred Heart." This introduction to a new school would once again give Fr. de Boylesve a sign regarding the future work he would one day accomplish, although on this occasion he did not know it at the time. He made his first vows at the Maison du Passage on October 10, 1833. He studied philosophy and then in 1835 became a supervisor at the Collège de Mélan, a position he held for one year. He remained in the same college until 1842 where he was in succession professor of grammar, humanities and rhetoric. He thoroughly enjoyed his work with the students, writing in 1837:

"I find this job a lot of fun, despite the hardships that come with it. I have forty students; I love them and I try to spare nothing to make them good Christians, educated Christians capable of one day rendering true service to religion and to the state. It is the sight of such a noble ending that sustains and animates me." In the same letter he continues, regarding his concern for his family, "(...) what the only important thing is, is everyone behaving well and does he remember the motto of the family, RELIGIO, PATRIA? For me who gave up everything, even my name which will be extinguished in my person, I remember it, and God grant that I am consumed and that I use myself in the service of one and of the other."

Although renouncing his aristocratic life he never gave up its noble spirit represented by the family motto, an ardent loyalty to the Catholic faith of his forefathers and his country. In the title pages of his texts he included the family crest of three crosses and motto: RELIGIO, PATRIE – "Faith and Country". Those who knew him and his 'military' style ways said he was just like the loyal intrepid knights of old.

At the end of 1842 he returned to France. He took theology courses at Laval for four years. Instinctively he was drawn to the writings of St. Thomas Aquinas and steered clear of new systems that deviated from the philosophical teachings of the Seraphic Doctor. In 1846 theology training completed, Fr. Boylesve was sent by his superiors to Angers, then in his third year at Notre-Dame d'Ay. In 1848 he was appointed to Brugelette, where he occupied the chair of philosophy. One student who fondly recalled Fr. de Boylesve and his time at Brugelette said his arrival was providential. His classes were easy to follow his manner clear and crisp, but this is not all that gained the respect of the students. In 1848 they were restless as revolution was in the air, Louis-Philippe I, who had overthrown Catholic King Charles X was now in his own turn overthrown. Rising above and beyond what was required of his philosophy courses, Fr. Boylesve seized the opportunity like a knight-commander of old to direct the lazy students yet bursting with energy towards something constructive: Catholic action to fashion them into vigorous young men of service for Church and country. With his apostolic action he captivated the students with his literature classes, speaking on many subjects from philosophy, history, politics both ancient and modern. He particularly drew them with his catechism lessons on the Council of Trent, his clarity and enthusiasm captivating them.

As Fr. de Boylesve loved his students he was equally admired and loved by them, earning the nickname 'The Captain' as a mark of respect. The students composed a military style tune for his birthday, the refrain remaining popular and hummed everywhere: "Courageous Captain, lead us into battle." A student recalls: "I understood all that was apostolic about his action on us. We can sum it up by saying that he made it his mission to preach to us always and everywhere the contemplation of Saint Ignatius on the Reign of Jesus Christ as it is given in the Exercises." In 1851 Fr. Boylesve was sent to Vannes where he was made prefect of studies, his nickname 'The Captain' following him. In October 1853 he left the post and resumed teaching philosophy, a position that he would keep for a long time, either in Poitiers or in Vaugirard.

Known to be quiet and reserved when on his own, it was another matter when he was teaching or publicly speaking. He was incapable of remaining silent or softening his direct manner of expression when it was a question of truth, and did not hold back when it came to defend the Faith and the Church against unbelievers, becoming as noted like his knight-ancestor of old, charging forth to give chase and defeat any bold rascal on the field of battle albeit with his tongue and writings rather than with a literal sword. His attitude is quaintly summed up by the art critique he once gave of the statue of the fountain of St. Michael in Paris, complaining with slight annoyance that the mighty archangel was made to look too carefree and benevolent when dispatching Satan: "See then, it is that he seems to spare him!" He was also a zealous worker and relished activity. He once wrote: "I challenge my superiors to give me too much work." In addition to his religious duties and teaching, he was a prolific writer, his output seeming to have no end. He wrote on a myriad of subjects and in different genres, from devotional booklets and pamphlets to history, literature, philosophy, Biblical dramas, summaries of the Church Fathers and Doctors, his own sermons, studies of the Scriptures, Our Lady, the Exercises of St. Ignatius just to name a few, there were always more plans for further works in progress, his room filled with notes and notebooks. He was always studying as well, also making it a practise to read through the entire Bible every year. One might call him a workaholic in today's terms, but it was noted he believed in a time and a place for everything and diligently managed his hours. He enjoyed recreation time, especially going for walks, and did not sacrifice rest. Despite his zest for work, he disapproved of a few young professors who sacrificed too much sleep and recreation time for their studies, endangering their health. Yet, while sparing of his time, he was ever charitable and ready to help another all for the glory of God.

In September 1870 Fr. de Boylesve was sent to the College of Le Mans, Notre-Dame de Sainte-Croix, when the Franco-Prussian war was raging and France suffered the indignity of invasion. The humiliation felt by the country also struck the pious and patriotic Fr. de Boylesve to the core: "I searched through the memories of my life; I do not remember ever having felt greater pain than this, not even when I learned of my mother's death. This humiliation of France, the Eldest Daughter of the Church, thus succumbing before Prussia, the Eldest Daughter of Protestantism, in the face of the whole world, is something unheard of."

The Messenger, the magazine of the Apostleship of Prayer run by the Jesuits, began spreading the visions of St. Margaret Mary, declaring the only way France would be saved from her enemies was to embrace the devotion to the Sacred Heart. The message inspired Fr. de Boylesve. He became a chaplain to the Catholic Papal Zouaves forces sent to defend the French Motherland from the Protestant invaders, giving them rousing sermons: "Clotilde, inspiring faith in Clovis, saved the Franks and slaughtered the Germans at their feet ... Joan of Arc by her standard delivered France from the English! Your standard is the Sacred Heart." The Zouaves placed the Sacred Heart on their banner. Fr. de Boylesve also busily spread Sacred Heart badges of wool for the soldiers to pin on their uniforms, for they were in high demand. A gifted and inspiring preacher, his sermons encouraged them onward, even when they were driven back in defeat by the Prussians to where the soldiers remarked: "This man can lead us to the fire tomorrow; we would gladly be killed for him."

Fr. de Boylesve is fondly remembered today in Catholic circles in France for his work as the director of the Apostleship of Prayer in Le Mans through which he contributed to the spread of devotion to the Sacred Heart. On October 17, 1870 Fr de Boylesve was appointed to preach at the Visitation of Le Mans upon St. Margaret Mary for his subject, who at the time was a Blessed. He also preached upon another mystic who had died within their own times, Mother Marie de Jesus (1797-1854) from the convent des Oiseaux of Paris who had received revelations from the Sacred Heart that were favourably recognised by the Archbishop of Paris. On June 21, 1823 the Sacred Heart revealed to Sr. Marie that He desired France be consecrated to His Sacred Heart by the King, and that a chapel be built and dedicated to Him, and the feast of the national consecration be formally celebrated every year. "After my sermon," recounts Fr. Boylesve, "the Mother Superior expressed to me her astonishment at my silence with regard to an almost similar order that Our Lord had given to Blessed Margaret Mary on

June 17th, 1689. I confessed that in our college, which had barely opened for a month, I had not found the letters of the Blessed One and that I was unaware of the apparition and the order she was telling me about. I promised to make good this omission." Apparently at that time, the Sacred Heart's requests to St. Margaret Mary for a shrine and the national consecration of France by the King were not yet widely known.

True to his word, filled with his characteristic zeal for faith and country, doing what he could to extend the reign of Jesus Christ through his beloved homeland and secure its safety, the very next day he repaired his omission by publishing a pamphlet featuring the prophecies of St. Margaret Mary and Mother Marie de Jesus entitled "Triumph of France by the Sacred Heart", composing a special prayer of consecration to be said, which the Zouaves said every Friday as hope in the Sacred Heart was sorely needed. Paris was threatened with destruction by bombardments, then starvation by the invading Prussians, having commenced a siege around the city in September 1870. The siege continued until January 1871, the citizens reduced to dire circumstances. The zoo animals were slaughtered for food, the populace also living off of stray animals and rats. While the Prussian advance had ceased, humiliation still ensued when France suffered defeat at the hands of the Prussians with the establishment of the German Empire, also losing the territory of the Alsace-Lorraine to the victors. The troubles were not over. From March to May 1871 Paris fell into the clutches of the anticlerical socialist Communards, rebels revolting against the new government of the Third Republic. Blood ran in the streets, historical buildings burned, including the Tuileries Palace. The anticlerical Communards also executed the Archbishop of Paris, Georges Darboy, fulfilling the prophecy of St. Catherine Laboure. This horrific turn of events, combined with the circulation of prophecies foretelling the destruction of Paris was at hand, the faithful no doubt felt doom hung over the city. The times were desperate. After several reprintings, including a full reproduction of the text by Fr. Ramiere in the 'Messenger' newsletter issued by the Apostleship of Prayer, more than 330,000 copies of Fr. de Boylesve's pamphlets of the 'Triumph of the Sacred Heart' were circulated. It contributed to the rapid spread devotion to the Sacred Heart and bolstered the call to have the Universal Church consecrated to the Sacred Heart, also to build a national shrine on Montmartre in atonement for the atrocities committed by the Communards who began their uprising there. Construction began in 1875, the cornerstone was laid on June 16, 1875, the day Bl. Pius IX encouraged all the faithful to pray the consecration to the Sacred Heart using the special formula composed by the Sacred Congregation of Rites for the 200th anniversary of the apparition of the Sacred Heart to St. Margaret Mary. The construction of Sacre Coeur was at last completed in 1914.

As for Fr. de Boylesve, he continued to spread devotion to the Sacred Heart in other works, notably, this beautiful edition explaining the relationship of the Divine Heart within the Holy Trinity, the Church, the Sacraments and the Seven Gifts of the Holy Spirit with examples taken from the Holy Scriptures. Also, judging from the context of the wording of the Consecration of France at the end this work, it is no doubt the same special prayer he composed for the Papal Zouave forces and which they said every Friday for the salvation of France.

In addition to his efforts to spread devotion to the Sacred Heart of Jesus, he worked unceasingly at many other endeavours, not only as director of the Apostolate of Prayer in Le Mans, but also with the Confraternities of Saint Joseph such as that of the Good Death, and also the Confraternity of the Agonizing Heart, the Work of Campaigns, Conferences of St. Vincent de Paul, Workers' Circles, he still appeared to dare all and sundry that they would never be able to find enough work for him to do. He amazed all that he was never at a loss for a subject to preach upon. He could easily vary his sermons to where it appeared he never preached the same way twice, and always captured his hearers' attention. One day out of curiosity a hardened sinner walked in to listen to him preach and left a converted man. When Fr. Boylesve wasn't working, he was praying. There was no question that he maintained a deep spiritual life. He was transferred to Vaugirard in 1875, returning to Le

Mans two years later in 1877. Three years later his teaching came to an end at the college there with the decree of March 29, 1880 issued by the French minister for public education prohibiting the Jesuits from engaging in their educational apostolate, only the first of several anticlerical laws that would be passed in France over the next decades. Fr. Boylesve admitted he was on the verge of tears saying his last Mass for the students in the chapel before the school closed. Yet, he remained as active as ever despite this terrible blow, preaching, giving catechisms and continuing his writing, tackling the problems of their day threatening both the Church and society. He continued working despite his old age, until the end of 1891 when his activity was curtailed. He was struck with various ailments, first a tormenting dermatitis that remained with him, then inflammation of the blood that restricted his activities for many weeks, although he managed to say Mass and continue his writing, until at last he was struck with paralysis, unable to walk or speak. Clutching his rosary and his crucifix, the ever zealous 'priest-knight' of the Vendée gave up his soul to God in February 22, 1892 and was buried in the Jesuit cemetery of Sainte-Croix.[1]

1   Biographical information from 'Necrologie. Le Père Marin de Boyleseve, in 'Lettres de Jersey', Vol.XII, No. 1 (April 1893)

The Heart of Jesus in the Gospel

Only God exists by Himself. Everything comes from God. God is the Father, Principle of all that is. God is the Son: He is the Word from which God knowing Himself, affirms Himself. God is the Holy Spirit: He is the Love by which God desires and loves Himself, and through which He gives being to what was not.

The Word Made Flesh

And the Word was made Flesh, the Son of God was made the Son of man. He took a body and a soul like ours in the womb of the Virgin Mary. God made man is called Jesus Christ.

And the Holy Spirit poured out all His gifts in the Soul of Jesus. And the Soul of Jesus is light by intelligence and flame by will. The soul thinks with the help of the brain in which it imprints the image of its ideas. It loves, with the help of the heart to which it communicates its impressions, its affections, its aversions, its love or its hatred.[*]

---

[*] Note, Fr. De Boylesve is speaking of the action of the human heart in general, it can love or hate. However, there is also a 'hatred' for all that is evil; not a sinful hatred, but a holy and just detestation of everything that is evil. The Heart of Jesus certainly felt

On entering the world, at the moment of His Incarnation, Jesus said to His Father from the depths of His Heart: "Thou hast refused the host and the ancient oblation, but Thou hast given Me a body; the burnt offerings for sin have ceased to please Thee. So I said, 'Here I am coming; at the head of the book, at the beginning of everything it is written of Me that I will do, O God! Thy will.'[++] In this first act, in this sacrifice to the Good Divine pleasure sums up the whole Heart of Jesus.

The Nativity

The Infant was born, the angels sang: "Glory to God in the highest, and on earth peace to men of good will." (Luke 2:14) Unite, O men! Unite your wills with the Will of the Infant Jesus, your hearts to His Heart, and you will want what God wants, you will love what God loves. Such is order, and order is peace: *Tranquillitas ordinis*. (The tranquillity of order.)[O]

---

such a holy detestation. "The fear of the Lord hateth evil: I hate arrogance, and pride, and every wicked way, and a mouth with a double tongue." (Proverbs 8:13)

[++] Fr. de Boylesve is referring to this prophetic passage in Psalm 39 (7-8): "Sacrifice and oblation thou didst not desire; but Thou hast pierced ears for me. Burnt offering and sin offering Thou didst not require: Then said I, Behold I come. In the head of the book it is written of me. That I should do thy will: O my God, I have desired it, and Thy law in the midst of my heart."

[O] St Augustine provides a definition of *Tranquillitas*

The Circumcision

Eight days pass. The Infant is circumcised, the Blood flows. It is the Heart which imprints on the Blood this movement by which life circulates in the whole body. This Infant will be great: *hic erit magnus*, ("He will be great", Luke 1:32) for His Heart will shed all His Blood for the salvation of the world. To this great Heart must respond the Name which is greatness *par excellence*: this name is Jesus.

The Presentation

Forty days have passed since the birth of the Infant. Joseph and Mary present Him at the Temple. The sacrifice is approved by the Heavenly Father. The elderly Simeon announces that this Infant will be the focal point of contradictions, and that consequently a sword of

---

ordinis in his *'City of God'*, Book 19, that is, meaning the "tranquillity of order" or "well-ordered concord", "the peace of all things". Peace is order, order in which all things in the universe have their proper place established by God their Creator. Peace is therefore the state a person or thing achieves when it is in accordance with the larger created order. Fr. de Boylesve shows that we cannot have true order or peace unless we are united with the Heart of Jesus.

sorrow will pierce the Heart of His Mother. But the Heart of Jesus will be pierced by the spear.

His Hidden Life

At twelve years old, Jesus hides away from the tender solicitude of his parents. Mary addresses a sweet complaint to Him, the Child offers only one excuse: He had to be entirely about the interests of the glory of His Father. Jesus reveals all His Heart in this word.

His Public Life

For three years Jesus proclaims the Kingdom of Heaven. We know that the mouth speaks from the abundance of the heart.[#] The Gospel, the Good News, therefore comes from the Heart of Jesus.

[#]   "For out of the abundance of the heart the mouth speaketh." (Matthew 12:34) Also, Luke (6:45).

The Passion

The hour of the Passion is about to strike. At the sight of the bitter chalice, at the sight of the suffering and humiliations of the cross, at the sight of the ingratitude of the wicked who will persist in losing themselves, and of the indifference of His own who sleep while the traitor watches, the so sensitive and so generous Heart of Jesus is raised up with pain; however, He accepts the bitter chalice and cries out: "May Thy will be done, O My Father, and not Mine!" But with this effort, the repressed Blood violently escapes through all the pores and forms a bloody sweat, the drops of which flow to the ground, *Initia dolorum haec:* ('These things are the beginning of sorrows.' Mark 13:8), for this Sacred Heart, this is only the beginning of the sorrows.

The Cross

On the cross Jesus will die. He cries out. This cry perhaps announced the rupture of His Heart. And if so, as some scholars believe, Jesus would have therefore died of pain and love. At the sight of the uselessness of His cross for the millions of souls who will reject grace, at the sight of the carelessness or cowardice of so many

of His most devoted servants, the Heart of Jesus is broken. And this crushing of the Divine Heart provokes the terrible cry which announces the last breath of the Saviour.

The Lance

He is dead. A strike of the lance opens His side. Blood and water escape from His broken Heart. The Water represents baptism which purifies, the Blood represents the Eucharist which vivifies. These two sacraments, one of which is the first and the most necessary, and the other the most excellent, constitute the Christian and the Church. As Eve, mother of the human family according to nature came out from the side of Adam while plunged into a deep sleep, so the Church, mother of the human family according to grace, came out of the Heart of Jesus while sleeping the deep sleep of death. Children of the Heart of Jesus, seek life at the Source from where we received it, we will not find it elsewhere.

Devotion to the Sacred Heart

Here then is this Heart which has loved men so much! For this wounded Heart, broken much more by ingratitude and indifference than by the blow of the lance, Jesus demands a special devotion which consists of two main acts: reparation of honour or honourable amends, and consecration.

This devotion must be exterior and interior. As an outward sign of reparation Jesus asks for a special feast in honour of His Divine Heart, the Friday after the octave of the Blessed Sacrament. This day must be sanctified by Communion and by an honourable amendment. Every Friday of the year and especially the first Friday of each month should be dedicated to the Heart of Jesus, as they already are to the memory of the Passion, which is summed up in this Divine Heart.

The Image of the Sacred Heart

Jesus also wants His Heart to be represented by an image. He asks for a church in which a picture will be placed where the Divine Heart will be painted. He promises the most abundant blessings to all who display the image of His Sacred Heart in their home and to those who carry it with them.

It seems obvious that the Heart of Jesus should be represented as it was shown by Jesus Himself to Blessed Margaret Mary.

Often Jesus bared His chest and showed His Heart opened by the lance and letting out torrents of flame. This image is difficult to execute. We can imagine that Jesus, showing His transparent chest like crystal, shows His visible Heart in the place it actually occupies in the human body. But neither drawing nor painting can easily convey this view. Also most of the paintings represent the Heart of Jesus, drawn or painted, not on the inside of the chest, but on the surface and like a heart-shaped plaque applied to the body. This is not how Blessed Marguerite had the Heart of Jesus represented.[**] She had

---

[**] Note: While Fr. Marin thought images of Christ with His Heart applied 'outside' of His chest do not seem correct, this is his personal opinion here, and even he noted it would be difficult to represent what was in the vision! Artists are human and can only do their best.

This is how St. Margaret Mary described the Heart Itself, and apparently this is what should be represented as closely as possible: (July 2, 1674): "The Divine Heart was presented to me in a throne of flames, more resplendent than a sun, transparent as crystal, with this adorable wound. And it was surrounded with a crown of thorns, signifying the punctures made in it by our sins, and a cross above (...). This Heart of God must be honoured under the form of His Heart of flesh, whose image He wanted exposed."

Therefore, as long as the image of Christ and His Heart is clearly identifiable with these details given by St. Margaret Mary, the image is acceptable.

Him drawn and painted as He had appeared in several: alone, surrounded by a crown of thorns which does not touch Him, since on the head, it belongs to the heart only through the acceptance of it. The cross seems to come out of the very Heart because from the moment Jesus entered this world, the cross was implanted in His Heart. The wound made by the lance is visible, and flames escape through this opening, as well as the upper opening.

The Heart of Jesus and the Trinity

Now let us study the Divine Heart Itself and seek to enter It.

The Heart of Jesus is like the Centre of the world and the summary of all things. Under the action of the August Trinity It exerts Its influence over all creation. In this first study we will consider It in Its relationship with the Father, the Son and the Holy Spirit; in another study we will be able to indicate Its relations with creatures and above all with man, whom It is its complement and abridgement.[&]

ജ ♥ ൙

[&] Unusual expression, possibly Fr. de Boylesve meant the creation of mankind can be concisely summed up in the Heart of Jesus.

I. The Heart of Jesus and the Father

The mouth speaks from the abundance of the heart. (Matthew 12:34. Luke 6:45)

The prayer that Jesus taught us was therefore obviously the one that continually escaped from His Heart.

Our Father, Who Art in Heaven

Pater: 'Father, thou art My Creator* and therefore my Lord and my King.' This was the expression of the sentiment of the Heart of Jesus, when He contemplated God as the Creator.

Pater: 'Father, Thou art the Father of the Word to which My Soul and My Body are so intimately united, of the Word which by My Soul vivifies Me, animates Me and fills Me with the lights of truth and the flames of charity.' This was the cry of the Heart of Jesus when He beheld

---

*   It is obvious Fr. Marin did not mean Jesus was 'created' as Christ was eternally begotten of the Father before all ages and not made. No doubt Fr. Marin intended to point out Christ in *general* was praising God the Father as Creator. Christ assumed human nature that was created. As the Son of Man, the God-man, in His Heart He praises God His Father as the Creator.

God as the First Person and First Principle in the Blessed Trinity.

Pater noster: Our Father, 'Thou art not just My Father, because I am not just Thy Word and as such not just Thy only Son; I am man, I am the Son of man, I am the Son of Mary, and through her the Son of Adam. I am therefore the Brother of all the sons of Adam, and since Thou art My Father, Thou art also the Father of all My brothers according to human nature. Thou art their Father with Me and with the Holy Spirit as Creator; Thou art also their Father as Thou art also Mine. I am Thy only Child by Divine nature; but by grace and by adoption all men art Thy sons and My brothers. I will therefore not only say to Thee; 'My Father', but I say to Thee: '*Our* Father.' This was the prayer of the Heart of Jesus for us, in whom He loved to recognize and consider His brothers.

Qui es in coelis, Who art in heaven. *Sursum corda,* ("Lift up your hearts") let us raise our hearts high. Heaven is the abode of the Father; there He shows Himself in the brilliance of His glory; this is our homeland. Let us say those impulses of the Heart of Jesus, since from His lips these words so often escaped: 'My Heavenly Father, thy Father Who art in Heaven', He sees thee and will reward thee.

Like Jesus and with Jesus let us dwell in Heaven by heart, by spirit, by thought, by intention, by desire, by affection.

Hallowed be Thy Name

Sanctificetur nomen tuum: A son takes to heart the honour of the paternal name. The great, perpetual preoccupation of the Heart of Jesus is the glory of His Heavenly Father. *Manifestavi nomen tuum hominibus*: ("I have manifested thy name to the men," John 17:6) to manifest and thereby glorify the Divine Name, such is His passion, his Work. *Opus ejus coram illo*. (" ... and his work is before him." Isaiah 62:11). Our Father's Name is our name. The injury done to the Name of God is an injury done to ourselves. If we are the brothers of Jesus and the children of the heavenly Father, like Jesus we will take the Holy Name of God to heart. Our hearts will be indignant at the mere thought of the blasphemies of the press and of the impious schools. We will join forces to exterminate ungodly teaching, whether given verbally or in writing, by school or by book, by club or by newspaper; we will oppose ungodly propaganda with the propagation of good books, and we will leave no stone unturned to defend the honour of the sacred Name of our Father Who is in Heaven.

Thy Kingdom Come

Adveniat regnum tuum, Thy kingdom come. The reign and kingdom of the Heavenly Father is Heaven, it is the whole world, it is the Church, it is the heart of every Christian, it is above all the Heart of Jesus. Prime Creator,*** and therefore supreme Lord and King of all that exists, the Heavenly Father reigns over the Soul of Jesus; the Soul of Jesus, by His very Will conforms to that of the Father, *quae placita sunt ei facio semper,* ("I do always the things that please him." John 8:29) It governs His Heart, and by His Heart all His passions, all His senses, all the members of His Body. From the Heart of Jesus, united to His Soul and to the Word, emanates the action by which He governs each man in particular, each family, each nation, the entire great human society. Woe to the man, woe to the family, woe to the nation, woe to that royalty which would not allow itself to be governed by the Heart of the King of kings, Who received from the Father all power on earth as in Heaven: *gens enim et regnum quod non servierit tibi peribit*; ("For the nation and the kingdom that will not serve thee, shall perish," Isaiah 60:12), every nation, every royalty that will not have served Thee will perish! On the contrary, honour and happiness to those who will allow

*** i.e. God created all things from nothing. The Prime Mover as St. Thomas describes Him.

40

themselves to be governed - governed by the royal and Divine Heart of the unique Supreme King! The reign of the Father transports Heaven to this earth. So Jesus taught us to ask that the Kingdom of the Father comes to us on earth as it is in Heaven. Therefore let us allow ourselves be ruled on earth by the Heart of Jesus like the angels and saints in Heaven, and we will find Heaven on this earth.

Thy Will be Done

Fiat voluntas tua, Thy Will be done. It will be done. All that God wills is done: *quaecumque voluit fecit*. ("He hath done all things whatsoever he would." Psalm 113:11)[+] Therefore wanting what God wants is the secret of strength and greatness. Here also is summed up all the perfection of the Heart of Jesus, like that of the Heart of Mary: and it is by this continuous *fiat* that our heart will find itself conforming to the Divine Heart.

[+]   Also compare with Psalm 134:6 - "Omnia quaecumque voluit Dominus fecit," - 'Whatsoever the Lord hath pleased he hath done,' according to the Douay-Rheims translation. It could also be translated as: "All things whatsoever the Lord willed He did."

The Fiat of the Creation

God said: *fiat lux*! ("Be light made." Gen. 1:3) Let there be light and the light shined. At this word, repeated six times, from nothingness comes forth being, from out of chaos comes forth the world. *Dixit et facta sunt.* ("For he spoke and they were made," Psalm 32:9). He spoke, it is done; that first *fiat* is the first outward manifestation, the first expression of the Divine Word. It is the same Word which took a soul and a body like ours in the womb of the Virgin Mary. This Soul and this Body are summed up in a sense in His Heart, and just as the heart of man is in the centre of the body, the centre of the circulation of the blood and there even of life, it is the centre of the whole man, and also, as the organ of love, the final end of all the powers of the soul and the principle of all passions, and consequently, of all human action. Thus the Heart of Jesus, Word made flesh, God made Man, is the centre of all of Creation, the supreme expression and the first intention of the Creator's *fiat*. Under the impulse of the human will, so perfectly in accordance with the Divine Will, this Sacred Heart is the main instrument of Divine Action in the order of creation and providence, in the order of sanctification and of grace, in the order of glorification and glory. Everything that the Father, the Son and the Holy Spirit thought and wanted arrives through the Soul of Jesus to His Sacred Heart, and from this Heart starts the movement, the action, the Word which governs the world, which saves and that vivifies. But to form this Heart, another *fiat* was needed.

The Fiat of the Incarnation

Fiat mihi secundum verbum tuum: be it done to me according to thy word. (Luke 1:38) To this *fiat* of faith, obedience and humility, the Word was made flesh and annihilated in Mary's womb.[*] But this annihilation is the masterpiece of wisdom, of goodness, of the power of God; it is the closest union that can exist between the Creator and the creature, between God and man, and by man between God and the world; it is the completion, the crowning of the creative *fiat*. And it is from the Heart of Mary that this Masterpiece comes because it is from the Heart of Mary that this *fiat* comes forth, it is from the Heart of Mary where this very pure blood escapes from which the Body of Jesus is formed by the operation of the Holy Spirit. And it is the Heart

---

[*] 'Annihilate' – i.e. that God 'emptied' or completely humbled Himself in becoming man. "But emptied himself, taking the form of a servant, being made in the likeness of men, and in habit found as a man." (Phil 2:7)

of Jesus which sums up the whole Incarnation. It is to the Heart that all the Blood arrives, it is from the Heart that the Blood leaves to vivify the whole Body, and it is in the Heart where all the affections, all the desires, all the resolutions of the Soul end. It is from the Heart that all the impulses, all generous devotion, all great designs and all great thoughts come from! Do you want proof? Follow Jesus to the Garden of Olives. There you will hear this generous prayer from His Heart: *Non mea voluntas, sed tua fiat* (Luke 22:42). "Not My will, but Thine be done."

The Fiat of the Redemption

Non mea voluntas, sed tua fiat (Luke 22:42). ("Not My will, but Thine be done".) It is the *fiat* of the Passion, the *fiat* of redemption, the *fiat* of sacrifice, the *fiat* of reparation.

Jesus subordinates His human will to that of His Father, and we look towards that of His Father, and we discover that it is just, as it should be. Why then do we have so much difficulty in sincerely saying our daily *fiat*: Thy will be done? Ah! It is because of the lack of courage, it is because our hearts fail us.

And yet this *fiat* is Heaven. Yes, may Thy Name be sanctified, Our Father! That Thy kingdom come, that Thy will be done on earth as it is in Heaven. This triple request contains the

44

triple condition without which there is no happiness possible here below.

Our Daily Bread

Panem nostrum quotidianum da nobis hodie. "Give us this day our daily bread." (Luke 11:3) It is again from the Heart of Jesus that this prayer comes forth. See around Him the multitude who followed Him into the desert. "I have compassion on the multitudes," Jesus said, "I will not send them away fasting." (Matt. 15:32) And His Heart, touched with pity, asks for the miracle of the multiplication of the loaves.

Thus, every day the Heart of Jesus asks for us the bread without which we would faint on the way. But if He asks for material bread for us, he asks with even more eagerness for the Bread of the soul.

This bread is first of all His Word and it comes from His Heart: the exterior word that He preaches and that He transmits to us without ceasing through His Church, the infallible echo of His own voice, and, by the interior word which enlightens us in the depths of the soul: *Nonne cor nostrum ardens erat ... .* "Was not our heart burning within us, whilst he spoke in this way," - Luke (24:32). Does not our heart blaze when, while on the road when we pass from one place to another, from one occupation to another,

Jesus speaks to us Heart to heart?

This daily bread is Jesus Himself present and hidden in the Eucharist. And it is again His Heart which inspired Him with this marvellous way by which He made Himself our daily Bread. Let us strive to fulfil the desire of such a generous Heart by frequent Communions, daily if possible.

Forgiveness

Dimitte nobis debita nostra, forgive us our debts, forgive us our trespasses, as we ourselves forgive our debtors what they owe us, as we forgive those who trespass against us. Head of this great body which is called humanity, Jesus regards Himself as charged with the crimes and offences of which His mystical body is guilty and from the bottom of His Heart He says to His Father: "Pardon as I pardon." And from the bottom of that Heart also emerges this word of forgiveness, this excuse in favour of those who have just had Him nailed to the cross: "Father, forgive them: for they know not what they do." (Luke 23:34) Such is the Heart of one who seems to say: "Learn by this generous forgiveness, learn of Me because I am meek and humble of heart." (Matt 11:29)

Temptation

Et ne nos inducas in tentationem. "And lead us not into temptation." Do not let us succumb to temptation. Certain of Himself,[+] the Heart of Jesus is not concerned here, but for us. Hence this prayer in which he identifies Himself with us, who are the members of a Body of which He is, and the Head and the Heart. At the moment of temptation let us therefore take refuge in this Heart as in a fortress, and while in the depths of this invincible Heart we will despise and we will reject both the seductions of the senses and the attractions of greed, and the mirage of vainglory. Were we like Jesus on the cross, abandoned so to speak by our Heavenly Father, we will repeat the cry that escaped from the Heart of Jesus, "My God, My God, why hast Thou forsaken Me?" (Matt 27:46) And soon our peace and confidence will be reborn despite the very excess of pain, and we will say again together with the Heart of our Saviour: 'My Father, I commit my soul into Thy hands, I abandon my dearest interests to Thee, I entrust to Thee all my sorrows. I no longer want to have any other concern than that of working and suffering for Thee.'

[+] 'Certain of Himself', that is, Christ cannot sin, and cannot succumb to the least temptation. His Heart, however, is concerned for us. He therefore taught us in the 'Our Father' to pray for help when temptations come.

Deliverance from Evil

Sed libera nos à malo. "But deliver us from evil." Touched by our evils which He takes on as His own and which He feels in His Heart as if they were personal to Him, and, speaking to His Father on behalf of His members who are Christians and are of His mystical Body that is the Church, Jesus asks for us deliverance from evil. Certainly sensible evils as He Himself asked for the removal of the chalice of the Passion, but above all the deliverance from spiritual evils: from error, which is the evil of the intelligence, and from sin, the evil of the will, and thereby deliverance from Hell, the punishment for sin. Hell, a misfortune that is absolute and eternal.

United in the Heart of Jesus, let us often repeat the requests of the prayer that He Himself taught us, and let us say with Him: 'Amen'. So be it!

⋙ ♥ ⋘

II. The Heart of Jesus and the Word

The Word is made flesh. He united Himself intimately and forever with the Soul and the Body which He took in the womb of Mary. Through the soul the body is vivified and animated. But it is through the heart by the blood that the soul itself causes to circulate both movement and life in the entire body.

In addition, in the soul there are two main faculties: intelligence and will. Intelligence corresponds to the brain, the head. The heart corresponds to the will. It is impossible to want without knowing, but once the will (heart) is set in motion by the intelligence (head), the former reacts on the latter. It is up to the will to apply intelligence to its object, to command attention and to maintain it. Therefore it has been said: 'Great thoughts come from the heart'; and again; 'The mouth speaks from the abundance of the heart.' Thought, therefore, although it is an act of the intelligence, depends on the will which keeps the intelligence applied and attentive. The word, (speech) depends even more on the will (heart), which at its will, commands people to speak or to be silent. In the end, action, which is the realization of thought just as speech is the expression of thought, depends absolutely on the will whose role is to order and to carry out the designs and plans conceived and ordered by the

intelligence. Now it is through the heart that the will executes all that is linked to external movement, such as words and actions. Words and action therefore start from the heart.

The Gospel and the Church

The Word of Jesus is called the Gospel, *Evangelium regni*: (Matt 4:23), the Gospel of the kingdom. This kingdom is the Church. The Church is the work, the principal action of Jesus Christ; it is the realization of His Word or His Gospel. The Church was therefore to come forth from the Heart of the Incarnate Word. And that is what happened. Jesus has just died. His Body is suspended from the cross. A soldier approaches, he strikes the side of Jesus, and with a blow of his lance he pierces the Heart. Immediately from this half-opened Heart escapes Water and Blood. The Water represents baptism. This sacrament is first before all the others, as it is the first (required) for the spiritual birth of a Christian, member of the Church. The Blood figures the Eucharist. This Sacrament is like the centre and the end of all the others; It is for the Christian the nourishment of the spiritual life, It is the bond and the union of the members of the Church.

We can therefore say that with these two sacraments all the others came forth from the

Heart of Jesus. Now the sacraments are precisely what constitutes the Church or the Mystical Body of Jesus Christ. It is through sacraments that Christians are members of Jesus Christ, that they may live His Life, that they are united to Him, and that in Him and through Him they are united among themselves so as to form only one body, one heart and one soul: *Cor unum et anima una*. "(And the multitude of believers had but) one heart and one soul," (Acts 4:32). Let us consider the sacraments through the Heart of Jesus, and we will recognize in them the relationship of this Sacred Heart with the Word Incarnate, Head of the Church.

Baptism

Baptism as we have said comes from out the Heart of Jesus with that Water which purifies by blotting out sin and which calms the fires of lust. Continue Thy work, O Divine Heart! Purify my heart and set it ablaze. The flame that comes from out Thy wound will extinguish the flame of sensuality. Submerged as if buried in Thy Heart and in Thy Blood, all robed and as if invested with Thee, I will live by Thee and like Thee, and I will every day be transformed more and more in Thee.

Confirmation

Confirmation emanates from the Heart of Jesus, Source of the anointing that softens and strengthens at the same time. "Learn of Me," the Saviour has said, "for I am meek and humble of heart." United with the Divine Heart we will be clothed with this strength and patience which endures the bellows, the insults, the whips, the thorns, the cross itself, which despises the contempt and the honours of the world, which counts as nothing the pleasure and the pain of the senses, which resists the threats and the seductions from the tempting spirit. In short, it is by union with the Heart of Jesus that the Christian is confirmed in truth and in justice.

The Eucharist

The Eucharist is the supreme effort of the Heart of Him Who loved His own to the end, beyond all limits, beyond death, inventing this new means of remaining with us until the end of time: *usque in finem,* in order to be present in our midst, in order to sacrifice Himself perpetually for us: *juge sacrificium*, "the continual sacrifice" (Daniel), in order to give Himself and to unite Himself with us in Holy

Communion by which He makes Himself our Bread, our Food, our Drink and our Life.

Sacrament of Penance

Penitence, again, comes to us the Heart of Jesus. It is from this Sacred Heart pierced by our sins which flows this salutary water of grace for repentance of the past and the firm purpose (of amendment) for the future. The Heart of Jesus broken by pain communicates to us the contrition that breaks our guilty heart. The Heart of Jesus, stronger than death, gives our purpose of amendment to sin no more the firmness of an invincible resolution.

As the Heart of Jesus was opened by the lance, so let us open our hearts and our consciences by our admission: a frank, sincere, humble and entire confession of our sins.

All the pains that Jesus endured in His Body and in His Soul during His entire life, and especially during His Passion, to atone and to repair for our sins, are concentrated and summed up in His Heart. This Divine Heart communicates to us our penitence, and the power and merit to make satisfaction before God. If, then, we wish to make reparation and atone for our faults, let us unite our weak merits with the infinite merits of the Sacred Heart.

Finally, it is from the Heart of Jesus

repeating for each of us: "Father, forgive them, they know not what they do," it is from this Heart so sweet and so merciful that comes the sentence of forgiveness which confirms the absolution of the priest and gives it its validity and its efficacy.

Extreme Unction

Extreme unction has as its source the Heart of Jesus from where the Divine Blood flows unceasingly, which was first of all for Jesus Himself the supreme and last unction. At the Garden of Olives Jesus was bathed in a sweat of Blood. By the scourging it is as though He is inundated with His own Blood. The thorns of His crown make His Blood flow over His eyes, ears, nostrils, lips. By the nails with which they are pierced, His hands and feet also receive the anointing of Blood. As it was for Jesus, agonizing first in the garden then on the cross, the last anointing is represented and recalled by the holy oils which draw all their strength and their value from the Blood that Jesus poured out for us in His Passion and the Water that the spear caused to gush from His Sacred Heart.

Holy Orders

Holy Orders confers upon the priesthood a triple power, the source of which is the Heart of Jesus. 1st power - to preach the Gospel. As we have said, the Gospel came from out of the Heart of Jesus, the Source of all great thoughts and of every good word: *pectus est quod disertos facit*;[**] 2nd power - to remit sins. This forgiveness comes from out of the Heart of Jesus, source of all mercy. 3rd, power - to consecrate and immolate Jesus on the altar. The sacrifice that Jesus made of Himself on the cross, and which is continually renewed in the Eucharist, proceeds from the love with which His Sacred Heart is set ablaze for the glory of His Father and for the salvation of souls.

[**]   Reference to a line in *De Institutione Oratoria* by Quintilian, "Pectus est enim quod disertos facit, et vis mentis." (Book X, Chapter VII, 15. "For it is the heart that makes eloquence (in speech), and gives power to the mind."

Marriage

Marriage is the sacred sign of the spiritual union of Jesus Christ with the Church. As Eve was drawn from Adam's side while he was sleeping a deep sleep, so the Church came out of the Heart of Jesus sleeping on the cross in the sleep of death; she the Church came out with the Water which represents Baptism and with the Blood which represents the Eucharist. We are therefore born of the Heart of Jesus by the spiritual generation of Baptism, we live by the Heart of Jesus by taking Holy Communion by the Eucharistic Bread. In our turn, let us work so that Jesus may be born in souls by the Water and the Blood, by word, by prayer, by preaching, by the example of our life, by sacrifice. And just as Jesus loves the Church as His Spouse, so children of the Heart of Jesus and of the Church, let us love her as our mother and may love of the Church be our dominant passion. This passion will extinguish all others, or transform them, and destroying the selfishness of self-love down to the root, it will make us men of heart, men of the Heart of Jesus, heroes and saints.

❧ ♥ ☙

III. The Heart of Jesus and the Holy Spirit

Conceived by the operation of the Holy Spirit, the Heart of Jesus is the masterpiece of the Sovereign Goodness and the most precious gift of Divine Love.

At that solemn moment of the baptism of Jesus when the heavens opened and the voice of the Heavenly Father was heard saying: "This is My beloved Son," the Holy Spirit in the form of a dove manifested His presence in the Sacred Heart, which from the first moment of Its existence was the place of His repose. (Isaiah 11: 2) ("And the spirit of the Lord shall rest upon him: the spirit of wisdom, and of understanding, the spirit of counsel, and of fortitude, the spirit of knowledge, and of godliness.")

Let us consider how the Divine Heart corresponds to each of the seven gifts of the Sanctifying Spirit.

The Gift of the Fear of God

There is a fear that never shakes the Heart of Jesus: it is the fear of the world, the fear of men. However it is written of Jesus that at the approach of the Passion He was afraid: *Coepit*

pavere. ("And He began to fear," Matt. 14:33) This valiant Heart, this Heart so strong therefore experienced fear for a moment. The anticipation of suffering and humiliation troubled Him and made Him tremble. It is because Jesus became man. The Word was made flesh and the flesh dreads suffering, as the soul dreads humiliation. But this fear of nature was overcome by supernatural fear, and if the Heart of Jesus could be troubled for a moment by fear, It was not shaken. He continued forward, resolved to endure everything for the glory of His Father and for the salvation of souls, after having said: *Transeat a me calix iste*: (Matt. 26:39), "My Father, may this chalice of sorrows and reproaches depart from my lips," Jesus added: "However Thy will be done and not Mine; let it be done, not as I will, but as Thou will." The fear of sin** therefore prevails in the Heart of Jesus over the fear of the pain; the fear of God triumphs over the fear of man.

Yes, the Heart of Jesus feared sin, not for Himself - He is impeccable - but for us who commit it so easily. He feared for us the double evil of sin; the evil of guilt, which is the spiritual

---

**   Again, we know Jesus cannot sin, so He did not fear to commit sin. Fr. De Boylesve shows that Our Lord was giving an example of the spiritual gift of the 'fear of God': to be willing to suffer anything rather than to go against His holy Will. Men due to human nature fear pain, but do not fear committing sin. We should fear to commit the least sin, and be prepared to do whatever God wills of us, even if it means to suffer. The cross is our salvation and leads to Eternal Life.

death of the soul by the loss of grace, and the evil of pain, hell and all its horrors, hell and its eternity. Wanting to deliver us from this double evil, in spite of the fears and the repugnance of nature, the Heart of Jesus accepted for Itself all the sufferings, all the humiliations of the Passion and the Cross.

The Heart of Jesus feared God, His Father. He was not afraid of displeasing Him. Was This not the Heart in which God the Father found all His satisfaction? But He feared the offences of our malice and of our weakness against the Divine Goodness; and to prevent them, at least to make reparation and atone for them, He accepted all the horrors of the Passion. It was to say to us: 'See how much sin is a great evil: sin offends the goodness of My Father, sin is an act in which man prefers a created good to the Supreme Good which is God, by which he prefers his own will to the Will of My Father, this Will so wise, so just, so good. When? O men! When will you realize that God is the only real Good and that you must sacrifice all other goods for It? When will you understand that the Will of My Father is so in accordance with wisdom, with righteousness, with absolute goodness? That all wisdom, all righteousness, all goodness consists in willing what My Father wills? To repair the crime and the madness of your sin, I accept the most dreadful evils. In order to make you understand that all these evils that I am going to suffer, frightful as they are, are nothing compared to the malice of mortal sin which offends the Divine Goodness and which contradicts the Divine Will. They are nothing compared to the eternal woe of hell to which you condemn yourself by sin.'

Such is the wondrous dedication that the gift of fear worked in the Heart of Jesus.

The Gift of Piety

Piety is that tender and strong love which leads a son to sacrifice himself for his parents, and a father, a mother to sacrifice themselves for their child. - Enter the Heart of Jesus. It is a temple in which the One continually offers Himself as a sacrifice, Who, through the cross and on the cross, owes God His Father the glory that sin had robbed Him of, and His brothers and sisters peace and salvation. Jesus was only nailed to the cross for a few hours; but the cross had been implanted in His Heart from the first moment of the Incarnation, and from that first moment, by the aspiration of His Heart, Jesus nailed Himself to this cross. It is because piety is not only a soft and tender feeling which leads one to pray to God, to remember His presence and His goodness; this gift includes above all the desire to devote oneself and to sacrifice oneself for the One Who is loved. We can even assure that a piety which is confined to praying, to that form of prayer which does not lead to one sacrifice themselves for the interests of God and for souls, would be a sterile and illusory prayer and piety.

Again, admire the piety of the Heart of Jesus for His Mother. With what tenderness He obeys her every wish: *Et erat subditus*; "And was subject (to them)," (Luke 2:51), how, at her prayer, He brought forward the time to grant His first miracle. With what solicitude from the height of his cross He entrusted her to the care of the beloved disciple!

The piety of this Divine Heart flows over all men. He has piety for the people who follow Him: *Misereor super turbam*; ("I have compassion on the multitude," Mark 8:2) He heals bodies, He instructs intelligences; He gives life to the body, He gives life to the soul. He compares Himself to a Good Shepherd who Himself seeks the lost sheep and brings it back to the fold on His own shoulders, to a loving father who happily receives a prodigal but repentant son. He weeps over His fatherland, over ungrateful Jerusalem. He forgives Magdalene, He cannot condemn the adulterous woman, and nailed to the cross He finds an excuse and asks forgiveness for His executioners.

The Gift of Knowledge

The gift of knowledge belongs to the mind; but as we have already observed, it also depends on the imprint which the will exerts on the intelligence. It is the mind that knows, and does know; but it is the will which applies the mind to an object or turns it away from it. We only know what we *want* to know. And the heart or the impassioned will, passion, love or hatred, exert a decisive influence on our ideas. We say; 'learn by heart', and the highest science is called wisdom, an expression which indicates the taste of things and indicates the intervention of the heart. We also say: 'philosophy is the love of wisdom' to designate the study of supreme knowledge, and the same word (φιλεώ) also means 'I love' and 'I study'. We study what we like, and we see, we understand, we judge things according to the inclinations of passion, and according to whether the heart stops the reason on such an aspect and such a relation rather than on another. And if it is true that the great thoughts come from the heart, Jesus also declares that from the heart comes human and criminal thoughts. Therefore the gift of knowledge is claimed by the Heart of Jesus, there is where we will find its fullness.

All we can know boils down to three things: God, the soul, and the world. Go to the school of the Heart of Jesus; there you will learn that God alone is the Supreme Good, and that therefore everything comes from God, everything returns to Him. One passion fills and possesses the Heart of Jesus; to make God His Father known and bring everything back to Him: *Manifestavi nomen tuum hominibus... . Tui erant, tu mihi eos dedisti... et mea omnia tua sunt and tua mea sunt*: "I have manifested Thy name to the men whom Thou hast given Me out of the world. Thine they were, and to Me Thou gavest them ... And all My things are Thine, and Thine are Mine," (John 17:6,10); all of His Father's interests become His.

Go to the Heart of Jesus, there you will learn what a soul is worth. The cross which emerges like a tree from the Sacred Heart emerges from Its germ, the thorns which crown this generous Heart, the Blood and the water which gush from It under the blow of the lance like a font of graces, these flames which escape from this furnace of Love, are so many signs which declare the price of the soul. To save one soul, this is what the Heart of Jesus wanted to suffer.

Go to the Heart of Jesus and you will know what the world is: a ladder to ascend to God, a way to know God, to love Him and to serve Him. Everything in the world that does not serve to elevate the soul to God, to make better known His power, His wisdom, His goodness, and consequently to make Him loved more, all that does not serve for that is useless. Everything that causes God to be forgotten, everything that turns away from God is disastrous. This is what the Heart of Jesus teaches us, sacrificing everything to free ourselves from the riches, the pleasures, the honours of the world and to raise us above the world by contempt of what the worldly ones esteem, by detesting what the world loves.

The Gift of Fortitude

The gift of fortitude immediately belongs to the heart. It is not enough to know, it is necessary to *act* in consequence of what one knows. Now it is from the heart that the energy for action begins, also the constancy that continues (the act), and the perseverance that ends it, all proceed from the heart. Upon entering this world Jesus said in His Heart: "Here I am; I am coming, O God! To do Thy will," and from the first moment of His existence[**] He offers Himself in sacrifice. However, neither the examples of His regular and common life in Nazareth, nor His preaching, nor His miracles lead to the conversion of the Jews; scarcely a small number of obscure people believed in His word and His mission. Nothing can discourage His constancy; He continues His work as if success crowned each one of His steps. Now what is the success of so many works, so many speeches, so many benefits and miracles? The Passion. This is where all His efforts to re-establish the kingdom of God on earth seem to lead and end. He perseveres, however, and even under the whips and under the crown of thorns, even on the cross, He calls Himself King, He calls Himself the Son of God. He will suffer

---

[**]   I. e. from the first moment of His 'existence' as God made man at the Incarnation.

everything, He will die rather than renounce His design. Such is the strength of this great and noble Heart; also His perseverance will finally triumph; His work will be accomplished. There is not one of His words that is not carried out. Through the cross He will conquer, He will reign, He will command, and, the gates of hell will not prevail against Him, against His Church, against the work of His Heart.

The Gift of Counsel

It does not suffice to know and want what is good. It is necessary to *achieve* it, and for that you have to know the means to get there. Fortitude by itself becomes a peril if it is not directed by the gift of council. This gift is a light which discovers the best means of attaining the end shown by the gift of knowledge and desired by the gift of fortitude. Council belongs to reason, but the ability to choose, even in view of the best means, often depends on the influence of the passions of which the heart is the seat and the organ. The heart influences the head. It is difficult to be a man of the mind if one is not a man of the heart. The gift of counsel therefore rests as much on the righteousness and firmness of the heart as on the rectitude and solidity of judgement, since these qualities of the spirit so often depend on those of the heart which we have just named.

Moreover, the end being God and His glory, the most effective means to glorify God are summed up in the three evangelical counsels: poverty, chastity, obedience. Now, this triple counsel came out of the Heart of Jesus as a lesson and at the same time as an example, and these three counsels require above all the intervention of the heart in order to be followed.

Jesus counsels poverty, voluntary poverty, openness of mind and heart, detachment from all these material goods which are chained to the earth and which stop our rising towards the only Supreme Good, towards God. Penetrate into His Heart and this Heart will tell you, even higher than His Word, the freedom, the royalty that results from voluntary poverty and disengagement from all that is material.

Jesus counsels chastity. "Blessed," He said, "are those who have a pure heart." Look at the Heart of Jesus: what purity in Its affections! What contempt for all sensible pleasure! What contempt for suffering![+]

Jesus counsels obedience. But obedience is impossible without meekness and humility. And where will you learn to be meek and humble, if not in the school of the Heart of Jesus. *Discite a me quia mitis sum and humilis corde.* "Learn of me, because I am meek, and humble of heart." (Matt. 11:29)

[+]   I.e. He had a holy contempt for the false crippling fear of pain and suffering that the world imparts, preventing one from doing the will of God. See again the section of the Gift of the Fear of God.

Obedience itself comes straight from the heart. Therefore, Jesus has the law of His Heavenly Father in the very midst of His Heart: *Deus meus, volui, et legem tuam in medio cordis mei.* ("O my God, I have desired it, and thy law in the midst of my heart." Psalm 39:9). Hear this cry of the Heart of Jesus reduced to agony by the effort of His heroic obedience: "Not what I will, but what Thou will, O My Father: *Non quod ego volo, sed quod ti.*" Then see Him walking to death, and penetrating more and more into this Heart so submissive, recognize with the Apostle that He made Himself obedient unto death and unto death on the cross. (Phil. 2:8) Here is the supreme counsel, the surest, the shortest way to glorify God, the one that contains all the others: *obedience.* Now if obedience is dictated by faith and reason, it starts from the will, it starts from the heart.

The Gift of Understanding

The gift of understanding adds to that of knowledge. We can know without understanding. I *know* there are Three Persons in One God, I don't *understand* this mystery. Like knowledge and counsel, understanding belongs to the mind; but if the passion which comes from the heart often becomes an obstacle to knowledge and counsel, it can also cloud the truth already shown by the gift of knowledge, or the better part (choice) recognized thanks to the gift of counsel.   It takes a *pure heart* to penetrate to the bottom of things and to grasp and *understand* what reason and faith have declared.

"Blessed," said the Saviour, "are those who have a pure heart, for they will see God." Let us unite our heart to the Heart of Jesus, and with Him enlightened by the Spirit of knowledge we will see God everywhere and in everything. It is in this intimate, deep, penetrating view that understanding especially consists.

Three principle books are open before us: the world, the Bible, the Cross.   These three books are summed up in the Heart of Jesus.

Enter the Sacred Heart, and you will understand that the world exists for us only in that we learn to emerge from this world to go back endlessly to God, which is recalled to us by all that strikes our senses here below.

The Bible is a closed book of which the Heart of Jesus is the key. The Old Testament announces the New. The New Testament is the union of man with God; first in Jesus, God-Man, then in ourselves united with Jesus. But this union remains inexplicable and unintelligible without the love which alone could compel a God to become man in order to save and raise up miserable sinners. This love with all its excesses, you recognize it, you see it, so to speak, made sensible in that Heart half-opened by the lance which completes the sacrifice.

The cross is even more unintelligible than the Incarnation of which the Bible is the announcement and the history. If a God became man, He should at least have surrounded Himself with all the splendours that enhance humanity! Already this God made man scandalizes us; what will it be like with a *crucified* God-man, delivered to all tortures, to all opprobrium?# Who will give me understanding of this third book which is a *cross*? The heart. Jesus loved men so much, He loved His Father so much for the salvation of men and for the glory of His Father that He did not only want to take on the form of a slave, but He humbled Himself, making Himself obedient unto death, and death on the cross. When I see Jesus suffering all the pains, all the humiliations to make reparation for sin and to atone, to give God the glory and man happiness, I understand that sin is a greater evil, a greater shame than all the suffering and all the humiliations endured by Jesus to repair it; I understand that God is so great and so good that everything must be sacrificed for Him; I finally understand what my soul is worth, since Jesus suffered so much to redeem it. Now the cross would not tell me any of this if it had been imposed by force; but when

---

Explanation: without the gift of understanding, the Incarnation and the birth of Christ seem inexplicable – that a perfect and All Powerful God would choose a poor life and to be born in a stable! Not a great palace! Hence this 'scandalizes us', i.e. those without understanding. So, how much more perplexing is it for God to choose a criminal's death on the cross, that is, when not seen with the gift of understanding. It is the gift of understanding that helps us see things as God sees them.

penetrating into the Heart of Jesus, I recognize that it is by a pure and free love that He accepts the torments and the ignominy of His Passion. I conclude that if He allowed Himself to be nailed to the cross is that He had the understanding of the malice of sin, understanding of the glory of His Father, of the value of our souls; that this understanding alone could inspire in Him a love stronger than death, than the death of the cross! So finally I begin to understand the cross, the suffering, the humiliation endured to make reparation for sin, to glorify God and to save souls.

The Gift of Wisdom

But we can understand *without having a taste for it*. What will give me a *delight* for the cross? The gift of wisdom.

Wisdom and knowledge of things through the highest causes. The highest cause is God, the First Principle and the Final End of all that is. To see God in everything, to see everything coming from God and returning to God, such is *speculative* wisdom. Wanting everything and expecting everything from God alone, wanting to give back everything to God alone, such is *practical* wisdom.

Speculative wisdom returns to contemplation, which is the most sublime act of understanding, since it is the repose of the understanding in God. Practical wisdom consists in the empowerment of love, which is the most sublime act of the will and its repose in God. Wisdom is therefore the perfect fulfilment of the need and that desire which perpetually torments the heart of man and which St. Augustine expressed in these terms: "For our heart is restless until it rests in Thee. *Irrequietum est cor nostrum donec requiescat in te.*" To see and love God in everything and everything in God, this is the end and happiness of man. In creating man and the world God proposed no other end, and if the happiness and the perfection of man is to know God and to love Him, the glory that God expects from man is to be recognized and loved as the Principle and the End of all good, and as the Supreme Good.

Enter the Heart of Jesus; there you will see only one desire, a single momentum. *Ascensiones posuit in corde.* ("In his heart he hath disposed to ascend by steps," Psalm 83:6) There is in the Sacred Heart a continuous movement of ascension, of elevation towards God the Father. Therefore He was advancing every day in wisdom before God and before men. To praise God, to glorify Him, to make Him known and manifest Him more and more, in order to make Him loved all the more, such therefore was the dominant and ever-growing passion of the Heart of Jesus, since the first moment of the Incarnation when the God-Infant exclaimed in the most intimate recesses of His

Heart: "You did not want, O God! The sacrifices of the old law, but you gave me a body, and I said, Here I am; I come to do your will,"* until that supreme moment when, uttering a loud cry, He surrendered His soul to His God. This cry came from a Heart broken by pain at the sight of the ingratitude and indifference of men. Jesus saw in advance the uselessness of His Passion and His death for so many millions of sinners who were to persist in losing themselves by refusing to return to God glory and love. We can say that the sole cause of the death of Jesus, the real blow that pierced His Heart, it was the criminal madness of the sinner preferring the creature to God, evil over good, or, which amounts to even preferring a finite and transient good to the Supreme, Infinite, Eternal Good. The Heart of Jesus was therefore like a Martyr for Wisdom. It had to be; for in descending on Jesus, the Spirit of Wisdom was only returning to the Heart of the Incarnate Word what He Himself receives eternally from the Divine Word, Who is Wisdom Itself from the Father.

---

*   "Wherefore when he cometh into the world, he saith: Sacrifice and oblation thou wouldest not: but a body thou hast fitted to me: Holocausts for sin did not please thee. Then said I: Behold I come: in the head of the book it is written of me: that I should do thy will, O God. In saying before, Sacrifices, and oblations, and holocausts for sin thou wouldest not, neither are they pleasing to thee, which are offered according to the law. Then said I: Behold, I come to do thy will, O God," (Heb. 10:5-9)

Consecration of France
to the Sacred Heart of Jesus

Jesus, Our Saviour and our King, here we are with the insignia of Thy Divine Heart, with the lance that pierced it, with the crown, with the cross, with Thy image fixed on our hearts, engraved on our crests and painted on our standards.

We have taken the spear, but it is no longer the spear that pierced the Heart of Jesus; we seize the lance to defend the Church born of the Divine Heart, when water and blood gushed out of It; water, symbol of Baptism, the Blood, symbol of the Eucharist. - Sons of the France of Clovis, we will be there, O Jesus, to defend the rights of Thy Heart and the liberty of Thy Church, we swear it and all together we will repeat:

"Heart of Jesus, we consecrate our hearts to Thee, we consecrate France to Thee."

Heart of Jesus, we shall be Thy crown. Too often we have been Thy crown of thorns, now we will be Thy crown of glory. Ranged around the August Head of the Church which, according to the language of St. Paul, is Thy body, ranged around Thy Vicar, our Holy Father the pope, we condemn all that he condemns, we affirm all that he asserts. We condemn error, all errors, every error; we affirm the Truth, all of the Truth, and nothing but the Truth. We swear to devote ourselves to the defence of the Truth; we swear to devote ourselves to the fight against error, and to attest to our resolution, all together we will repeat:

"Heart of Jesus, we consecrate our hearts to Thee, we consecrate France to Thee."

Heart of Jesus, we take up the cross, the cross reddened with Thy Blood, the cross of St. Peter, the cross of Constantine, the cross of the Crusades, the cross of St. Louis, greater in chains and through the cross than on his war horse and on his throne; we take the red cross that shone on the robes of Mary at the apparition of Pontmain, and here we are resolved to bear the cross with Thee, resolved to stand, with Mary, standing beside Thy cross, resolved to remain with Thee nailed to the cross, which means we are ready to suffer and die rather than betray Thy Heart and Thy Church. Because we are France, the true France, the Eldest Daughter of Thy Church and of Thy Heart, and together we will repeat:

"Heart of Jesus, we consecrate our hearts to Thee, we consecrate France to Thee."

Heart of Jesus, Thy will is to reign in the palaces: we have fixed Thy image in the palace of our heart. - Thy will is to be engraved on our arms, Thy will is to be painted on our standards: Thy image shines on our badges and on our banners.

Our banner will be the one which, leaving Paray, which rose in Paray; we sang and we will sing again the motto of this banner consecrated by the blood of the soldiers of the Pope and of France: Heart of Jesus, save France.

Heart of Jesus, Thy will is that France be consecrated to Thee, and Thou promised to fill her with Thy blessings. Already there is not a diocese which is not consecrated to Thee. Today, we, children of the true France, under the shadow of this flag, we cannot tire of repeating all together:

"Heart of Jesus, we consecrate our hearts to Thee, we consecrate France to Thee."

It is therefore done, Jesus Christ is our King and henceforth the flag of the Heart of Jesus will be the flag of France; let us cheer all together the Heart of Our Saviour and our King: Long live the Heart of Jesus!

It is Mary who brought us back to Jesus, it is through the Heart of Mary that we will reach the Heart of Jesus; Long Live the Heart of Mary!

And since it is through the humble Margaret Mary that Jesus revealed to us His Heart, let us say together: Long live Margaret Mary!

The Heart of Jesus, it is the Church. And the great affair of the Heart of Jesus, which is above all related to the Heart of Jesus, is the Church; and the Church is summed up in its head: *Ubi Petrus, ibi Ecclesia*; the Church today is Pius IX: Long Live Pius IX! - Long live the Pope-King!

And the Pope will be free[**] and the Pope will be king, when Catholics will have only one heart and one soul rallied around the standard of the Sacred Heart. And it is France which is and will be the standard-bearer of the Heart of Jesus – Long live France of the Sacred Heart!

80 ♥ ca

[**]　　　This consecration was written when the Papal States had been confiscated in 1870 under the pontificate of Bl. Pius IX. He and the popes after him were held as prisoners in the Vatican until the Lateran Treaty was signed in 1929, creating the Vatican City State.

Appendix

❦ ♥ ❦

Devotion to the Sacred Heart and the Nine First Fridays

Our Lord appeared to St. Margaret Mary (1647-1690) in a series of thirteen apparitions requesting she spread devotion to His Sacred Heart. On 27 December 1673, the feast of Saint John the Evangelist, she knelt at the the convent grill before which the Blessed Sacrament was exposed. Our Lord appeared to her and told her to take the place that Saint John had occupied at the Last Supper, and that she would act as His instrument. Jesus revealed His Sacred Heart as a symbol of His love for mankind, saying, "*My divine Heart is so inflamed with love for mankind ... that it can no longer contain within itself the flames of its burning charity and must spread them abroad by your means.*" She received another vision, which she describes July 2, 1674: "The Divine Heart was presented to me in a throne of flames, more resplendent than a sun, transparent as crystal, with this adorable wound. And it was surrounded with a crown of thorns, signifying the punctures made in it by our sins, and a cross above (...). This Heart of God must be honoured under the form of His Heart of

flesh, whose image He wanted exposed."

Through St. Margaret Mary, Our Lord had the Holy Hour established, and promised great graces those who practised to devotion to His Sacred Heart, and, who complete the Nine First Consecutive Fridays devotion in Its honour. To complete the Nine First Fridays, a person is to attend the Holy Mass and receive the Holy Communion. If the need arises, in order to receive Communion in a state of grace a person should also go to the Sacrament of Penance before attending Mass. In many Catholic communities the practice of the Holy Hour of meditation during the Exposition of the Blessed Sacrament during the First Fridays is encouraged.

ഇ ♥ ന

<u>The Twelve Promises of the Sacred Heart</u>

I will give them all the graces necessary for their state of life.

I will establish peace in their families.

I will console them in all their troubles.

They shall find in My Heart an assured refuge during life and especially at the hour of their death.

I will pour abundant blessings on all their undertakings.

Sinners shall find in My Heart the source of an infinite ocean of mercy.

Tepid souls shall become fervent.

Fervent souls shall speedily rise to great perfection.

I will bless the homes where an image of My Heart shall be exposed and honoured.

I will give to priests the power of touching the most hardened hearts.

Those who propagate this devotion shall have their names written in My Heart, never to be effaced.

The all-powerful love of My Heart will grant to all those who shall receive Communion on the First Friday of nine consecutive months the grace of final repentance; they shall not die under my displeasure, nor without receiving their Sacraments; My Heart shall be their assured refuge at that last hour.

೩ ♥ ೧

Enthronement of the Sacred Heart in the Home[+]

The practise of the Enthronement as a social crusade began in August 1907 at Paray le-Monial, France in the famous chapel of apparitions of the Sacred Heart inspired by the requests and promises of the Sacred Heart, especially: "I will reign through My Heart" and "I will bless every place where the image of My Heart is singularly honoured."

The Enthronement combines these two requests by installing prominently the image of the Sacred Heart as a sign of the acceptance of the reign of the Sacred Heart in the home. Founded by Mateo Crawley-Boevey, SS.CC, the movement was encouraged by several popes from St. Pius X to Pius XII. In a private letter to Father Mateo in 1917, Benedict XV gave formal approval to the Enthronement; this was renewed by Pius XII in 1948.

You may inquire at your church or parish to verify if the priest is prepared to do an Enthronement ceremony and has the official form, or, you may use the form below. The father or head of a family may also do the ceremony if it is impossible to have a priest preside.

[+] From in a booklet given the Nihil Obstat and Imprimatur, 1962.

Before the Ceremony

Set a date for the Enthronement in agreement with the priest. It is desirable to have a priest preside at the ceremony, but it is not essential to gain the indulgences. For serious reasons, the father, or someone else may preside and lead the prayers. In any case, please consult your parish priest.

If possible have the Holy Sacrifice of the Mass offered that morning for the reign of the Sacred Heart in your home, and as an act of love and reparation to the Sacred Heart. The entire family should try to receive Holy Communion at this Mass, or if that is not possible, at another Mass.

Obtain a picture or statue of the Sacred Heart according to the description of St. Margaret Mary as closely as possible. If you already have a picture, use that one.

Below the place of honour reserved for the statue or picture, prepare a "throne" or "altar," that is to say, a table, or perhaps the mantelpiece, covered with a white cloth, beautifully decorated with flowers and candles. The picture or statue should be placed on a small table near this "throne" before the ceremony.

Invite your relatives and friends to be present; thus you will already begin to be an 'apostle of the Sacred Heart.' Have a family celebration after the ceremony with a special treat for the children, who, of, course, should be present at the ceremony, including the youngest.

Make this day one of the outstanding events of the family life, one long to be remembered. The greater the solemnity, the better.

Note: Even if your home has already been consecrated to the Sacred Heart, you may still have the Enthronement, as the two are not the same.

The Enthronement Ceremony

1. All gather around the image of the Sacred Heart; father, mother and children nearest to the priest.

2. Priest, in surplice and white stole, blesses the image. (If no priest is present; have the image blessed beforehand.)

The Blessing of the Picture or Statue

In LATIN (translation below):

V. Adjutorium nostrum in nomine Domini.
    R. Qui fecit coelum et terram.
V. Dominus vobiscum.
    R. Et cum spiritu tuo.

Oremus. Omnipotens sempiterne Deus, qui sanctorum tuorum imagines pingi non reprobas, ut quoties illas oculis corporia intuemur, toties eorum actus et sanctitatern ad imitandum memoriae oculis meditemur, hanc quaesumus, imaginem in honorem et memoriam Sacratissimi Cordis Unigeniti Filii tui Domini Nostri Jesu Christi adaptatam bene ✠ dicere et sancti ✠ ficare digneris; et praesta ut quicumque coram illa, Cor Sacratissimum Unigeniti Filli tui suppliciter colere et honorare studuerit, illius meritis et obtentu a te gratiam in praesenti, et aeternam gloriam obtineat in futurum. Per Christum Dominum nostrum. Amen.

Translation:

V. Our help is in the name of the Lord.
    R. Who made Heaven and earth.
V. The Lord be with you.
    R. And with thy spirit.

Let us pray.   Almighty and everlasting God, who dost approve the painting and sculpturing of the images of Thy Saints, so that as often as we gaze upon them we are reminded to imitate their deeds and sanctity; vouchsafe, we implore Thee, to bless ✠   and sanctify ✠   this image made in honour and in memory of the Most Sacred Heart of Thy only begotten Son, our Lord Jesus Christ; and grant, that whosoever in its presence, will suppliantly worship and honour the Most Sacred Heart of Thy only begotten Son, may obtain through His merits and intercession grace in this life and everlasting glory in the world to come. Through Christ our Lord. Amen.

(*The priest here sprinkles the image with holy water.*)

3. Then the father (or in his absence, the mother or some other member of the family) enthrones the image in the place of honour prepared for it. This is the symbolic act of Enthronement.

4. All stand while the Apostle's Creed is recited as an act of faith on the part of the family.

5.   Everyone is seated while the priest addresses a few words to those present, reminding the members of the family of what the

Sacred Heart expects from families which have acknowledged Him as King; recalling the magnificent promises of the Sacred Heart; urging the family to live its Enthronement and frequently to renew the act of consecration which they are about to make

.

6. All kneel, while the priest and the father (or father alone, or his representative) recite the official Act of Consecration.

(*NOTE: The consecration to be said is the official text composed by Father Ladislaus, SS.CC., and approved by St. Pius X, at the request of the Procurator General of the Congregation of the Sacred Hearts by Rescript of May 19, 1908. It was made obligatory to gain the indulgences of the Enthronement by a decision of the Sacred Penitentiary on March 1, 1918. [A.A.8. April 1, 1918, II. 154.] The New Regulations on Indulgences do not grant specifically an indulgence for the Ceremony, but on the Feast of the Sacred Heart, which is the Friday of the Octave Day of Corpus Christi, the Sunday of the Octave occurs after the Second Sunday of Pentecost, which places the Feast after the Third Sunday of Pentecost; a plenary indulgence is granted for reciting on the Feast of the Sacred Heart the Litany of the Sacred Heart, which can be included in the Ceremony. A plenary indulgence is also granted for reciting the following Traditional Consecration on the Feast of the Sacred Heart, which is different than the official Act of Consecration, but both are suitable and presented here. The Traditional first, the Official Consecration for the Enthronement is after it.)*

Act of Consecration of the Human Race: Traditional[++]

Most sweet Jesus, Redeemer of the human race, look down upon us humbly prostrate before Thy altar. We are Thine, and Thine we wish to be; but to be more surely united with Thee, behold each one of us freely consecrates himself today to Thy most Sacred Heart. Many indeed have never known Thee; many too, despising Thy precepts, have rejected Thee. Have mercy on them all, most merciful Jesus, and draw them to Thy Sacred Heart. Be Thou King, O Lord, not only of the faithful who have never forsaken Thee, but also of the prodigal children who have abandoned Thee; grant that they may quickly return to their Father's house lest they die of wretchedness and hunger. Be Thou King of those who are deceived by erroneous opinions, or whom discord keeps aloof, and call them back to the harbour of truth and unity of faith, so that soon there may be but one flock and one Shepherd. Be Thou King of all those who are still involved in the darkness of idolatry or of

---

[++] History of this particular Consecration prayer: on December 11, 1925, Pope Pius XI ordered that the consecration of the human race to the Sacred Heart should be renewed yearly on the last Sunday of October, the Feast of Christ the King. The consecration is to be made by reciting the Act of Consecration and the Litany of the Sacred Heart before the Blessed Sacrament exposed. An Indulgence of five years for each recital. The faithful who are present at the recital of this Act of Consecration before the Blessed Sacrament Exposed on the Feast of Christ the King may gain an indulgence of seven years, or, a Plenary Indulgence if they Have been to Confession and Holy Communion.

Islamism, and refuse not to to draw them all into the light and kingdom of God. Turn Thine eyes of mercy towards the children of that race, once Thy chosen people: of old they called down upon themselves the Blood of the Saviour; may It now descend upon them, a laver of redemption and of life. Grant, O Lord, to Thy Church assurance of freedom and immunity from harm; give peace and order to all nations, and make the earth resound from pole to pole with one cry: "Praise be to the divine Heart that wrought our salvation; to It be glory and honour for ever." Amen.

Official Act of Consecration to the Sacred Heart for the Enthronement

(Recited by the priest and the father together, or father alone, or representative, if no priest is present. At the time that this ceremony was approved by the Holy See, this Act was mandatory for the indulgence, but this indulgence has not been granted for this formula with the New Regulations.)

O Sacred Heart of Jesus, who didst make known to St. Margaret Mary Thine ardent desire to reign over Christian families, behold us assembled here today to proclaim Thine absolute dominion over our home.

Henceforth we purpose to lead a life like

unto Thine, so that amongst us may flourish the virtues for which Thou didst promise peace on earth, and for this end we will banish from our midst the spirit of the world which Thou dost abhor so much.

Thou wilt reign over our understanding by the simplicity of our faith. Thou wilt reign over our hearts by an ardent love for Thee; and may the flame of this love be kept burning in our hearts by the frequent reception of the Holy Eucharist.

Deign, O Divine Heart, to preside over our meetings, to bless our undertakings, both spiritual and temporal, to banish all worry and care, to sanctify our joys and soothe our sorrows. If any of us should ever have the misfortune to grieve Thy Sacred Heart, remind him of Thy goodness and mercy toward the repentant sinner.

Lastly when the hour of separation will sound and death will plunge our home into mourning, then shall we all and everyone of us be resigned to Thy eternal decrees, and seek consolation in the thought that we shall one day be reunited in Heaven, where we shall sing the praises and blessings of Thy Sacred Heart for all eternity.

May the Immaculate Heart of Mary and the glorious Patriarch St. Joseph offer Thee this our Consecration, and remind us of the same all the days of our life.

Glory to the Divine Heart of Jesus, our King and our Father!

Continuation of the Ceremony

7. The priest here asks those present to say with him an Our Father and Hail Mary for all the absent members, both living and dead, so that all may share in the graces of the Enthronement.

8. All recite with the priest (or head of the family) the following:

Prayer of Thanksgiving

Glory be to Thee, O Sacred Heart of Jesus, for the infinite mercy Thou hast bestowed upon the privileged members of this family. Thou hast chosen it from thousands of others, as a recipient of Thy love and a sanctuary of reparation wherein Thy most loving Heart shall find consolation for the ingratitude of men. How great, O Lord Jesus, is the confusion of this portion of Thy faithful flock as we accept the unmerited honour of seeing Thee preside over our family! Silently we adore Thee, overjoyed to see Thee sharing under the same roof the toils, cares and joys of Thy children! It is true, we are not worthy that Thou shouldst enter our humble abode, but Thou hast already reassured us, when Thou didst reveal Thy Sacred Heart to us, teaching us to find in the wound of Thy Sacred Side the source of grace and life everlasting. In this loving and trusting spirit we give ourselves to Thee, Thou who art unchanging Life. Remain with us, Most Sacred Heart, for we feel an irresistible desire to love Thee and make Thee loved.

May our home be for Thee a haven as sweet as that of Bethany, where Thou canst find rest in the midst of loving friends, who like Mary have chosen the better part in the loving intimacy of Thy Heart! May this home be for Thee, O beloved Saviour, a humble but hospitable refuge during the exile imposed on Thee by Thine enemies.

Come, then, Lord Jesus, come, for here as at Nazareth, we have a tender love for the Virgin Mary, Thy sweet Mother whom Thou hast given us to be our Mother. Come, to fill with Thy sweet presence the vacancies which misfortune and death have wrought in our midst.

O most faithful Friend, hadst Thou been here in the midst of sorrow, our tears would have been less bitter; the comforting balm of peace would then have soothed these hidden wounds, which are known to Thee alone. Come, for even now perhaps, there is drawing near for us the twilight of tribulation, and the decline of the passing days of our youth and our illusions. Stay with us, for already it is late, and a perverted world seeks to envelop us in the darkness of its denials while we wish to adhere to Thee who alone art the Way the Truth and the Life. Repeat for us those words Thou didst utter of old: "This day I must abide in this home."

Yes, dear Lord, take up Thy abode with us, so that we may live in Thy love and in Thy presence, we who proclaim Thee as our King and wish no other! May Thy triumphant Heart, O Jesus, be forever loved, blessed, and glorified in this home! Thy Kingdom Come! Amen!

9. (All stand) To thank the Immaculate Heart of Mary for the grace of the Enthronement, and to proclaim this loving Mother as the Queen of the home, all recite the **Hail Holy Queen**. (*If so desired, an Act of Consecration to the Heart of Mary may be added, and her image installed near the Sacred Heart.*)

Hail, Holy Queen - (Salve, Regina)

Hail, holy Queen, Mother of mercy; hail our life, our sweetness and our hope. To thee do we cry, poor banished children of Eve. To thee do we send up our sighs, mourning and weeping in this valley of tears. Turn then, most gracious Advocate, thine eyes of mercy toward us. And after this our exile show unto us the blessed fruit of thy womb, Jesus. O clement, O loving, O sweet Virgin Mary. Pray for us, O holy Mother of God, that we may be made worthy of the promises of Christ. (Partial Indulgence.)

10. Answer the priest, or, say the following:
Most Sacred Heart of Jesus: _Have mercy on us!_ (Say 3 times.)

Immaculate Heart of Mary: _Pray for us._

St. Joseph: _Pray for us._

St. Margaret Mary: _Pray for us._

(ALL) Glory to the Most Sacred Heart of Jesus forever and ever! Amen.

11. The priest gives his blessing: May the blessing of Almighty God, Father, Son and Holy Spirit, descend upon you and remain forever. Amen.

12. Then the members of the family and the priest sign the Certificate of the Enthronement, which should be framed and hung near the image of the Sacred Heart or kept in the family vault. After the ceremony, send in name and address of family to a Local Center or to the National Center that records Enthronements of the Sacred Heart. Give date of ceremony, name of officiating priest, if any, and parish.

(*End of the Enthronement Ceremony*)

ଛ ♥ ଓ

Litany of the Sacred Heart of Jesus

Lord, have mercy.
> Christ, have mercy.

Lord, have mercy.

Christ, hear us.
> Christ, graciously hear us.

God, the Father of Heaven, *have mercy on us*.
God, the Son, Redeemer of the World,
have mercy on us.
God, the Holy Ghost, *have mercy on us*.
Holy Trinity, one God, *have mercy on us*.

Heart of Jesus, Son of the Eternal Father,
have mercy on us.
Heart of Jesus, formed in the womb of the Virgin
Mother by the Holy Ghost,
have mercy on us.
Heart of Jesus, united substantially with the
word of God, *have mercy on us*.
Heart of Jesus, of infinite majesty,
have mercy on us.
Heart of Jesus, holy temple of God,
have mercy on us.
Heart of Jesus, tabernacle of the Most High,
have mercy on us.
Heart of Jesus, house of God and gate of heaven,
have mercy on us.

Heart of Jesus, glowing furnace of charity,
have mercy on us.
Heart of Jesus, vessel of justice and love,
have mercy on us.
Heart of Jesus, full of goodness and love,
have mercy on us.
Heart of Jesus, abyss of all virtues,
have mercy on us.
Heart of Jesus, most worthy of all praise,
have mercy on us.
Heart of Jesus, king and centre of all hearts,
have mercy on us.
Heart of Jesus, in whom are all the treasures of
wisdom and knowledge,
have mercy on us.
Heart of Jesus, in whom dwelleth all the fullness
of the Divinity, *have mercy on us.*
Heart of Jesus, in whom the Father is well
pleased, *have mercy on us.*
Heart of Jesus, of whose fullness we have all
received, *have mercy on us.*
Heart of Jesus, desire of the everlasting hills,
have mercy on us.
Heart of Jesus, patient and rich in mercy,
have mercy on us.
Heart of Jesus, rich to all who invoke Thee,
have mercy on us.
Heart of Jesus, fount of life and holiness,
have mercy on us.
Heart of Jesus, propitiation for our sins,
have mercy on us.

Heart of Jesus, saturated with revilings, *have mercy on us.*

Heart of Jesus, crushed for our iniquities, *have mercy on us.*

Heart of Jesus, made obedient unto death, *have mercy on us.*

Heart of Jesus, pierced with a lance, *have mercy on us.*

Heart of Jesus, source of all consolation, *have mercy on us.*

Heart of Jesus, our life and resurrection, *have mercy on us.*

Heart of Jesus, our peace and reconciliation, *have mercy on us.*

Heart of Jesus, victim for our sins, *have mercy on us.*

Heart of Jesus, salvation of those who hope in Thee, *have mercy on us.*

Heart of Jesus, hope of those who die in Thee, *have mercy on us.*

Heart of Jesus, delight of all saints, *have mercy on us.*

Lamb of God, who takest away the sins of the world, *spare us, O Lord.*

Lamb of God, who takest away the sins of the world, *graciously hear us, O Lord.*

Lamb of God who takest away the sins of the world, *have mercy on us.*

V. Jesus, meek and humble of Heart.
     R. Make our hearts like unto Thine.

Let us pray

Almighty and everlasting God, look upon the Heart of Thy well-beloved Son and upon the acts of praise and satisfaction which He renders unto Thee in the name of sinners; and do Thou, in Thy great goodness, grant pardon to them who seek Thy mercy, in the name of the same Thy Son, Jesus Christ, who liveth and reigneth with Thee, world without end. Amen.

ℰ ♥ ℛ

Act of Reparation to the Sacred Heart of Jesus

(By the Encyclical of May 8, 1928, Pope Pius XI ordered that each year on the Feast of the Sacred Heart this Act of Reparation should be solemnly recited in all the churches of the world. An indulgence of five years for each recital. The faithful who assist at the recital of this Act of Reparation before the Blessed Sacrament exposed on the Feast of the Sacred Heart of Jesus may gain an indulgence of seven years, or, a plenary indulgence if they also have been to Confession and Holy Communion.)

Most sweet Jesus, whose overflowing charity for men is requited by so much forgetfulness, negligence and contempt, behold us prostrate before Thee, eager to repair by a special act of homage the cruel indifference and injuries to which Thy loving Heart is everywhere subject.

Mindful, alas! that we ourselves have had a share in such great indignities, which we now deplore from the depths of our hearts, we humbly ask Thy pardon and declare our readiness to atone by voluntary expiation, not only for our own personal offences, but also for the sins of those, who, straying far from the path of salvation, refuse in their obstinate infidelity to follow Thee, their Shepherd and Leader, or, renouncing the promises of their baptism, have cast off the sweet yoke of Thy law.

We are now resolved to expiate each and every deplorable outrage committed against Thee; we are determined to make amends for the manifold offences against Christian modesty in unbecoming dress and behaviour, for all the foul seductions laid to ensnare the feet of the innocent, for the frequent violations of Sundays and holy days, and the shocking blasphemies uttered against Thee and Thy Saints.

We wish also to make amends for the insults to which Thy Vicar on earth and Thy priests are subjected; for the profanation, by conscious neglect or terrible acts of sacrilege of the very Sacrament of Thy Divine Love; and lastly for the public crimes of nations who resist the rights and teaching authority of the Church which Thou hast founded.

Would, O Divine Jesus, that we were able to wash away such abominations with our blood. We now offer, in reparation for these violations of Thy divine honour, the satisfaction Thou didst once make to Thine Eternal Father on the cross and which Thou continuest to renew daily on our altars; we offer it in union with the acts of atonement of Thy Virgin Mother and all the Saints and of the pious faithful on earth; and we sincerely promise to make recompense, as far as we can with the help of Thy grace, for all neglect of Thy great love and for the sins we and others have committed in the past.

Henceforth, we will live a life of unwavering faith, of purity of conduct, of perfect observance of the precepts of the Gospel and especially that of charity. We promise to the best of our power to prevent others from offending Thee and to bring as many as possible to follow Thee.

O loving Jesus, through the intercession of the Blessed Virgin Mary, our model in reparation, deign to receive the voluntary offering we make of this act of expiation; and by the crowning gift of perseverance keep us faithful unto death in our duty and the allegiance we owe to Thee, so that we may all one day come to that happy home, where with the Father and the Holy Ghost Thou livest and reignest, God, world without end. Amen.

Indulgenced Prayers

ဆာ ♥ ര

Prayer for the Reign of the Sacred Heart

"Sacred Heart of Jesus, Thy kingdom come."

(300 days indulgence, each time.
Pius X, June 29, 1906.)

Prayer for Knowledge of the Sacred Heart

"O Jesus, Thou, Eternal Life in the bosom of the Father, Life of souls who are created after Thy own Image, by Thy love I beseech Thee, let us know Thy Divine Heart; reveal it to us."

(300 days indulgence, once a day.
Pius X, March 11, 1907)

Acts of Love and Praise

"All for Thee, most Sacred Heart of Jesus."

*(300 days indulgence, each time.
Pius X, Nov. 26, 1908)*

♥

"All praise, honour and glory
to the Divine Heart of Jesus."

*(50 days indulgence, once a day.
Leo XIII, June 14, 1901)*

♥

"Praised be the most Sacred Heart of Jesus.
Praised be the Immaculate Heart of Mary."

*(300 days indulgence, for each of these prayers
when used in saluting one another.
Pius X, May 30, 1908.)*

♥

"May the Sacred Heart of Jesus
be loved everywhere."

(100 days, once a day. Pius IX, Sept. 23, 1860)

♥

"O Heart of Jesus burning with love for us, inflame our hearts with love for Thee."

*(100 days indulgence, once a day.
Leo XIII, July 16, 1893)*

♥

"Sweet Heart of Jesus, be my love."

(300 days, once a day. Leo XIII, May 21, 1892.)

♥

"O sweetest Heart of Jesus, I implore that I may ever love Thee more and more."

*(300 days indulgence every time.
Pius IX, Nov. 26, 1876.)*

♥

"Blessed be the most loving Heart of Jesus and the most sweet Name of Our Lord Jesus Christ, and of Mary His most glorious Virgin Mother, forever and evermore."

(300 days indulgence, once a day, and, plenary indulgence once a month under the usual conditions. Pius X, Nov. 30, 1905)

Act of Humility

"Jesus meek and humble of heart,
make my heart like unto Thine."

*(300 days indulgence, each recitation.
St. Pius X, Rescript Sept. 13, 1906)*

Acts of Faith, Trust and Hope

"Sacred Heart of Jesus, I trust in Thee.

(300 days indulgence each time. Plenary
indulgence once a month, under the usual
conditions. Pius X, June 27, 1906)

♥

"Sacred Heart of Jesus,
I believe in Thy love for me."

*(300 indulgence days each time.
Pius X, July 29, 1907.)*

♥

O Heart of Love, I place all my trust in Thee, for though I fear all things from my weakness, I hope all things from Thy mercies."

(300 days indulgence each time,
Pius X, June 3, 1908)

Prayer for Mercy

"Most Sacred Heart of Jesus, have mercy on us."

(7 years, 280 days for making this invocation three times after Mass. Pius X, June 17, 1904.)

Mercy for Sinners

"Sweet Heart of Jesus, have mercy on us and on our erring brethren."

(100 days indulgence every time,
Pius X, Aug. 13, 1908)

Prayer for Purity

"Heart of Jesus, source of all purity,
have pity on us."

(100 days indulgence, Pius X, May 23, 1912.)

Act of Thanksgiving

"Honour, love and thanksgiving
to the Sacred Heart of Jesus."

(100 days indulgence. Pius X, Jan. 8, 1908)

Prayers for the Pope and the Church

"Lord Jesus, protect with Thy Divine Heart
our Holy Father, the Pope."

*(300 days indulgence, every time.
Pius X, April 10, 1907)*

♥

"Most Sacred Heart of Jesus, shower copiously Thy blessings on Thy holy Church, on the Supreme Pontiff, and on all the clergy; grant perseverance to the just, convert sinners, enlighten infidels, bless our parents, friends and benefactors; assist the dying, liberate the souls in purgatory, and extend over all hearts the sweet empire of Thy love."

(300 days indulgence, once a day. Plenary indulgence, once a month. Pius X, June 16, 1906)

♥

"Divine Heart of Jesus,
convert sinners, save the dying,
deliver the holy souls from purgatory."

*(300 days indulgence very time.
Pius X, Rescript July 13, 1906.)*

Sacrificial Prayer to be Said by Religious

"Heart of Jesus, Victim of love, make me for Thee a living sacrifice holy and pleasing to God."

*(50 days indulgence every time.
Pius X, Feb. 27, 1907)*

Prayer for in Times of Need

"O most compassionate Jesus! Thou alone art our salvation, our life and our resurrection. We implore Thee, therefore, do not forsake us in our needs and afflictions, but, by the agony of Thy most Sacred Heart, and by the sorrows of Thy Immaculate Mother, succour Thy servants whom Thou hast redeemed by Thy most Precious Blood."

(100 days indulgence, once a day.
Pius IX, Oct. 6, 1870)

Consecration of Reparation Prayer

"My loving Jesus, out of the grateful love I bear Thee, and to make reparation or my unfaithfulness to grace, I, (N.N.), consecrate myself wholly to Thee; and with Thy help I purpose never to sin again."

(100 days indulgence, once a day, if prayed before a picture of the Sacred Heart. Plenary indulgence once a month. Pius VII, June 9, 1807.)

Another Offering of Reparation

"Divine Heart of Jesus, through the compassionate Heart of Mary, I offer Thee all the prayers, all the works, and all the sufferings of this day, to atone for all the offences committed against Thee. All this I offer according to the intentions Thou dost constantly have at Thy Sacrifice on the altar."

(7 Years and 280 days indulgence, as often as said at Mass during the Novena to the Sacred Heart. Pius X, Nov. 15, 1907)

A Daily Oblation Offering
to the Sacred and Immaculate Hearts

"O Lord Jesus Christ, in union with that Divine intention with which Thou didst on earth offer praises to God through Thy Sacred Heart, and now dost continue to offer them in all places in the Sacrament of the Eucharist, and wilt do so to the end of the world, I most willingly offer Thee, throughout this entire day without the smallest exception, all my intentions and thoughts, all my affections and desires, all my words and actions, that they may be conformed to the most Sacred Heart of the Blessed Virgin Mary ever Immaculate."

*(100 days indulgence, once a day.
Leo XIII, Dec. 19, 1885.)*

Prayers to the Eucharistic Heart of Jesus

"Behold, my most loving Jesus, to what an excess Thy boundless love has carried Thee! Of Thine own Flesh and Blood Thou hast made ready for me a Divine Banquet in order to give me all Thyself. What was it that impelled Thou to this transport of love? It was Thy Heart, Thy loving Heart. O Adorable Heart of my Jesus burning furnace of Divine Love, within Thy most Sacred Wound receive Thou my soul, that in that school of charity I may learn to requite the love of that God Who has given me such wondrous proofs of His love."

(100 days indulgence, once a day. Pius VII, Feb. 9, 1818.)

♥

"Heart of Jesus in the Blessed Sacrament, burning with love of us, inflame our hearts with love of Thee."

(200 days indulgence each recitation, Leo XIII, Feb. 6, 1899)

♥

"Praised and blessed by the most Sacred Heart and the Precious Blood of Jesus in the Most Blessed Sacrament."

(100 days indulgence, once a day. Pius X, Aug. 25, 1908).

♥

"Blessed be the most
Holy Eucharistic Heart of Jesus."

(300 days indulgence each time. Pius X, June 12, 1905)

♥

"May the Heart of Jesus in the Most Blessed Sacrament be praised, adored and loved with grateful affection, at every moment, in all the Tabernacles of the world, even to the end of time. Amen."

(100 days indulgence, once a day.
Pius IX, Feb, 29 1868).

♥

"Let us with Mary Immaculate adore, thank supplicate and console the most Sacred and beloved Eucharistic Heart of Jesus."

(200 days indulgence each recitation,
Pius X, Dec. 19, 1904)

♥

"Eucharistic Heart of Jesus, have mercy on us."

(300 days indulgence each time.
Pius X, Dec. 26, 1907.)

♥

"Praised by the most Sacred Heart of Jesus in the Most Holy Sacrament."

(100 days indulgence each time. Pius X, July 11, 1914)

♥

"Eucharistic Heart of Jesus, increase in us our faith, hope and charity."

(300 days indulgence, each time. Benedict XV.)

Eucharistic Heart Prayers for Priests

"O Jesus, annihilated in the Holy Eucharist to be the home of love of the Catholic Church, and the strength of soul, we offer Thee our prayers, our actions, our sufferings, for Thy priests and in order that the reign of Thy Sacred Heart may be spread every day more and more."

(300 days indulgence once a day. Benedict XV, April 8, 1919.)

♥

"Eucharistic Heart of Jesus,
model of the priestly heart, have mercy on us."

*(300 days indulgence each time.
Pius X, Sept. 11, 1907).*

ଛ ♥ ଔ

FINIS

*"I go to prepare a place for you.
I Myself shall be your reward."*

Illustration Credits

Page 24. "Sacred Heart", Portuguese School, 19th Century.

Page 28. "Christ as a boy displaying his Sacred Heart." Engraving by A. Baratti after P. Monaldi. (c. 1760s). Wellcome Collection, public domain.

Page 31. "Adoration of the Sacred Heart", print by Thomas Kelly, 1874. Photograph from the Library of Congress, public domain. https://www.loc.gov/item/99401403

Page 36. "Los santos bajo la Santísima Trinidad, con el Sagrado Corazón de Jesús en medio", (1754) by Corrado Guaquinto. Public Domain. Wikimedia Commons.

Page 50. "Jesus the True Shepherd" print by Thomas Kelly, 1874. Photograph from the Library of Congress, public domain.

Page 54. "Sacred Heart suspended over a Chalice", engraving in the Wellcome Collection, public domain.

Page 59. "Sacred Heart of Jesus" (c. 1705) by Robert de Longe. (Desc. angels lifting many hearts up to the Sacred Heart). Wikimedia Commons, listed as public domain.

Page 61. *"The Sacred heart of Jesus. , 1882."* [Boston: Publisher Not Transcribed] Photograph from the Library of Congress, public domain. https://www.loc.gov/item/2018697554/.

Page 69. "Ángeles adorando el Corazón de Jesús" by Vincent López Portaña, (c. 1795). Wikimedia Commons, public domain.

Page 78. "An image of Christ showing his Sacred Heart is crowned by angels." Lithograph. Wellcome Collection, public domain.

Page 83. Jesus Christ. (Sacred Heart giving a Blessing), ca. 1877. [Philadelphia: Publisher Not Transcribed] Photograph. Library of Congress, public domain. https://www.loc.gov/item/2018697551/.

Page 85. "The apparition of our Lord to blessed Margaret Mary Alacoque", (Print, New York, c. 1900). Library of Congress, no known restrictions.

Page 88. "Christ presenting the Sacred Heart". Engraving by Francesco Rosaspina. Wellcome Collection, public domain.

Page 105. "Srce Jezusovo" by Ivan Grohar (c. 1900). (Wikimedia – listed as public domain.)

Page 108. "The Pietà with Christ's Sacred Heart appearing on his chest." Engraving. (1881) Wellcome Collection, public domain.

Page 112. "Our Lady of the Sacred Heart", (1910) Anon. (Wikimedia Commons, listed as public domain.)

Page 120. "Sacred heart of Jesus" , ca. 1880. [Boston: Publisher Not Transcribed] Photograph. Library of Congress, public domain. https://www.loc.gov/item/2018697552/.

Page 127. Allegory of doves flying through the Church to the Sacred Heart. (Date?) Wellcome Collection, public domain.

If you liked this book, you may also enjoy these by Fr. Marin de Boylesve

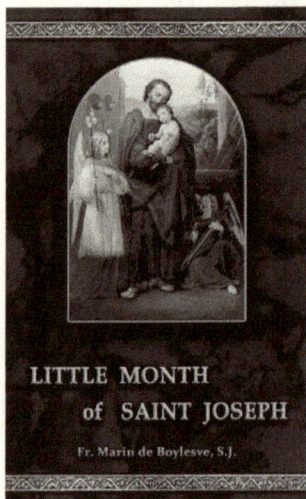

**Little Month
of Saint Joseph**

ISBN: 978-989-96844-8-5

**The Month of
Saint Michael**

ISBN: 978-989-96844-92

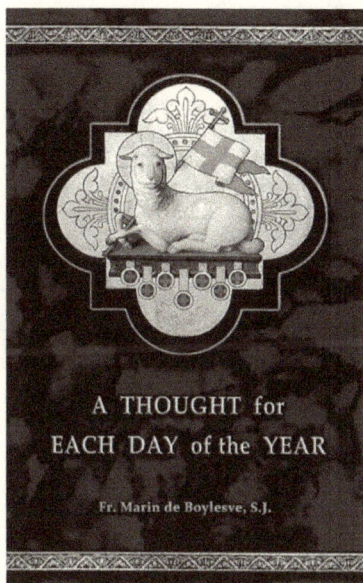

A THOUGHT for
EACH DAY of the YEAR

Fr. Marin de Boylesve, S.J.

A Thought for
Each Day of the Year

ISBN: 978-989-33-1995-6